The Giants of the Bible

THE GIANTS OF THE BIBLE

Leta Marie Lusk

VANTAGE PRESS
New York Washington Atlanta Hollywood

FIRST EDITION

Published by Vantage Press, Inc.
516 West 34th Street, New York, New York 10001

Manufactured in the United States of America
Standard Book Number 533-03247-4

I dedicate this book to my parents William Wesley and Ida Bowen Chaney. They taught me from childhood, to love and honor God, and His word, the Bible. To my three children Willard Lusk, Dennis Lusk, and daughter Deanna Grayson.

I have taught them to make a place in their hearts for God and His Holy word.

Our three generations have read the Bible and made many intensive studies. May the following generations do likewise.

Contents

Figures and Maps

FIGURES

MAPS

Preface

The book of *The Giants of the Bible* is unique in that it has the quotations from the Bible, leaving the reader free of looking up scriptures to prove its contents. It is also unique in having its own maps, for area information for each chapter, leaving the reader free of locating areas mentioned in map searching. Also unique in the dates of each chapter is the time date span, since creation.

All Bible scriptures are taken from the King James version of the word of God. The material for this book was either Bible scriptures, or the theory of the author herself. All maps and pictures used are the products of the author herself.

The picture of each person, depicting the garments worn by the person of the date, is in each chapter.

The subject seems to be a very interesting one, because of the mystery of the giants. In this book the Bible scriptures tells us all about the giants. Who they were, why they were upon the earth, the time, where they lived, and died.

Foreword

I am a Bible student for the sole purpose of enjoyment and the pleasure of reading God's inspired word. Having read the Bible through many times, I became so thrilled, and inspired to pursue a subject through the Bible until I feel the information on that particular subject has been exhausted.

I have been a Sunday school teacher for twenty-seven years. Having explored many Bible subjects with many delightful levels of age groups, from junior high to senior adult classes.

My desire in writing this book is that people may accept it as a proven source of knowledge from the Bible. To show the Bible speaks of an abundance of facts on many subjects, and that the reader might become interested in reading the word of God for themselves.

To my knowledge this subject has not been written about before. I pray the Holy Spirit of God will help each reader to enjoy reading this book, as I have enjoyed writing it.

Leta Marie Lusk

The Giants of the Bible

CHAPTER ONE

The Angels Sired the Giants Myth

The first mention of the giants in the Bible is in Genesis 6:4: There were giants in the earth in those days, and also after that, when the sons of God came in unto the daughters of men, and they bare children to them, the same became mighty men which were of old, men of renown.

There is a teaching that giants were the offsprings of angels, as they went in unto the daughters of men, the children were giants. Let us examine the part of Genesis 6:4 as to who the sons of God are.

Adam was the son of God as declared by Luke 3:38: Which was the son of Enos, which was the son of Seth, which was the son of Adam, which was the son of God.

Jesus was declared to be the son of God in Luke 3:22: And the Holy Ghost descended in a bodily shape like a dove upon Him, and a voice came from Heaven which said, "Thou art my beloved son, in thee I am well pleased." John 3:16 also declares Jesus to be the son of God. "For God so loved the world, that He gave His only begotten son, that whosoever believeth in Him should not perish, but have everlasting life." Matthew 4:3,4: And when the tempter came to Him, He said, "If thou be the son of God, command that those stones be made bread." But He answered and said, "It is written, man shall not live by bread alone, but by every word that proceedeth out of the mouth of God." Jesus was declared son of God in II Corinthians 1:3: Blessed be God even the Father of our Lord Jesus Christ, the Fathers of Mercies, and to all comfort.

The children of Israel are called sons of God, in Hosea 1:10: Yet the number of the children of Israel shall be as the sand of the sea, which cannot be measured nor numbered; and it shall come to pass, that in the place where it was unto them, ye are not my people, there it shall be said unto them, "Ye are the sons of the living God." Job was declared to be one of the sons of God as a holy man. Job 1:6: Now there was a day when the sons of God came to present themselves before the Lord, and Satan came also among them. Please notice these sons of God did not meet in Heaven, as many people teach, but they met at a place on earth such as the temple of God, once a year. Job 2:1 and 2: Again there was a day when the sons of God came to present themselves before the Lord, and Satan came also among them to present himself before the Lord, and the Lord said unto Satan, "from whence comest thou?" And Satan answered the Lord, and said "From going to and fro in the earth, and from walking up and down in it." Notice Satan was on earth. Satan is not a son of God, as will be proven later as an angel. The Lord was not expecting him to come together with the sons of God, beause he asked him why he was there, or where he came from.

Job 38:7: When the morning stars sang together, and all the sons of God shouted for Joy. These sons of God were Job and other holy men. Stars are luminous bodies. Each has a name they sing, and praise God. Stars are not angels, or sons of God, they are an order of their own. John 1:12: But as many as received Him, to them gave He power to become the sons of God, even to them that believed on His name. Here we see Christians of New Testament time being called sons of God, other New Testament scriptures confirming this thought. Romans 8:14: As many as are led by the spirit are sons of God. Philippians 2:15: That ye may be blameless and harmless, the sons of God, without rebuke, in the midst of a crooked and perverse nation, among who ye shine as lights in the world. John 3:1 and 2: Behold what manner of love the Father hath bestowed upon us that we should be called the sons of God.

So in these Bible texts we see the sons of God are Adam, men of Israel, Jesus and the New Testament believers who have believed in the name of Jesus Christ. Only these people can be called sons of God, and not angels.

Men began to multiply: Genesis 6:1 and 2: And it came to pass, when men began to multiply on the face of the earth, and daughters were born unto them, that the sons of God saw the daughters of men that they were fair and took them wives of all which they chose. From these two verses we see the daughters were of sons of men. These were ungodly people, such as Cain's descendants. Cain was a rebel and never repented before God. His descendants were also ungodly. In the second verse we see the men who were choosing these beautiful women were Godly men, or men who had been taught to honor God by Adam's descendants, and through Seth's descendants. This includes the Israelites. It seems the ungodly men had a custom of taking all the wives they wanted. God had given Adam one wife and until Lamech, descendant of Cain, there is no mention of them having more than one wife. Also notice it was men (flesh-humans), not angels, who were choosing and taking wives. Genesis 6:4 says the offspring were men of renown; this means they were men of illustrious reputation, of old age, or became wise.

Genesis 6:4: The giants were already in the land.

This Scripture was written about 2469 B.C. after Adam was created. In a later chapter you will see when the giants first appeared.

When the sons of God came together before God, Satan came as an adversary not as a son of God. Satan had been cast out of heaven where God dwells, sometimes called the third heaven. Isaiah 14:12: How art thou fallen from Heaven, O Lucifer, son of the morning! How art thou cut down to the ground, which didst weaken the nations. In this verse Satan is called the son of the morning, he is not called son of God. Satan has been cast out of his original abode among the stars. He also lost his luminous beauty. His heart's desire is to rise above the earth, unto his place, the third heaven. (From which he fell.)

Jesus is the bright and morning star. Rev. 2:2-16: I am the root and offspring of David, and the bright and morning star. We see in the New Testament in our age Jesus is in the midst of our worship to God, just as he was in Job's day. (As God was in their midst.) Although we cannot see him, Satan is also in our (worship) presenting ourselves to God.

Let us go on to establish the fact, angels are spirits, and cannot gender with humans. Psalms 103:20 and 21: Bless the Lord, ye His Angels, that excel in strength, that do His commandments, hearkening unto the voice of His word. Bless ye the Lord all ye His hosts: ye ministers of His, that do His pleasure. Angels do the will of the Lord. They do not take their time for their own pleasures, they cannot go out of the presence of God, and marry daughters of men. In fact they cannot marry, as we see in Luke 20:33: Therefore in the resurrection whose wife of them is she? For seven had her to wife. Verse 34: And Jesus answered saying unto them, the children of this world marry, and are given in marriage. Verse 35: But they which shall be accounted worthy to obtain that world, and the resurrection from the dead, neither marry, nor are given in marriage. Verse 36: Neither can they die any more, for they are equal unto the angels; and are the children of God, being children of resurrection. In these verses we see, angels are spirits as well as the resurrected dead, godly people who will be the spirits like God is a spirit.

Jesus Christ is the only begotten of the Father; He was half spirit and half flesh. If the fallen angels that were with Satan could have had love affairs with the daughters of men, would they not still be doing the same thing today?

When we read Hebrews I:I through 1:8 we see Jesus and not the angels was the son of God. Hebrews I:I: God who at sundry times and in divers manners spake in time past unto the fathers by the prophets. Verse 2: Hath in these last days spoken unto us by His son, whom He hath appointed heir of all things; by whom also he made the worlds. Verse 3: Who being the brightness of His glory, and the express image of His glory, and upholding all things by His power, when He had by Himself purged our sins, sat down on the right hand of the majesty on high. Verse 4: Being made so much better than the angels, as he hath by inheritance obtained a more excellent name than they. Verse 5: For unto which of His angels said He at any time, thou art My son, this day Have I begotten thee? And again, I will be to Him a father, and He shall be to me a son. Verse 6: And again, when He bringeth in the first begotten into the world, He saith, and let the angels of God worship Him. Verse 7: And of the angels He saith, who maketh His angels spirits, His ministers a flame of fire. Verse 8: But unto the son He saith thy throne O God is forever and ever; a sceptre of righteousness is the sceptre of thy kingdom. Verse 13: But to which of the angels said He at any time, sit on my right hand, until I make thine enemies thy footstool Verse 14: Are they not all ministering spirits, sent forth to minister for them who shall be heirs of salvation?

We have established who the sons of God were. Also who the daughters of men were, and who the angels were.

Therefore, there is no reasonable thinking that in Genesis 6:4 angels mixed with human females and sired the giants. As mentioned earlier in this chapter, the giants were already upon the earth when this scripture was written.

Giants are human, flesh and blood earthlings. If they had been offsprings of angels they could never have died. Angels are immortal.

Remember

John 3:16: For God so loved the world, He gave His only begotten son. That whosoever believeth in Him; shall not perish, but have everlasting life. Verse 17: For God sent not His son unto the world; to condemn the world, but that the world through Him might be saved.

The blood of Jesus was the blood of His father. One drop of His blood could have covered the sins of the entire world.

CHAPTER TWO

The Nephilim

The first mention of giants was in Genesis 6:4: There were giants in the earth in those days; and also after that, when the sons of God came in unto the daughters of men, and they bare children to them: the same became mighty men, which were of old, men of renown. These giants were called Nephilim, of uncertain etymology (word tracing in history). We shall describe these first giants as creations of the Antediluvians, aboriginals.

There is no direct trace of a people of such abnormal stature. They seem to run in a scale from nine feet, to fifteen feet tall. Since these great, powerful, tall and mighty men did not descend from angels, let us try and find out who they did descend from. They were certainly humans of great stature.

Other translations in the Hebrew language are Heb, Gibbor, Rapha, Raphah, and Rephaim. In the beginning (4004 B.C.), God placed man (Adam) in the Garden of Eden. There He walked and talked with them. (Both man and woman.) When Adam and Eve sinned, God expelled them from the garden. Cain also was driven from the garden area, and from the face of God. Cain refused to repent of killing is brother Abel and return to his first status of a friend and follower of God.

Cain left the garden, to an area (place), east of Eden called the Land of Nod. This was about 3875 B.C; There he took his wife (a sister) with him. Gen. 4:14: And Cain went out from the presence of the Lord, and dwelt in the land of Nod, on the east of Eden.

From this union (marriage) came Enoch, from Enoch, Irad was born. From Irad, Mehijael, from Mahijael was born Methusael. And from Methusael, Lamech. By now we have seven generations.

Lamech took two wives. God had given Adam one wife. Lamech had broken the law of God in marriage. Lamech also killed a young man, as Cain had done many years before. Another law of God was broken, this was murder of another man.

These seven generations of people refused to repent and worship God. After this time God has given us no record, following the lineage of Cain, or his descendants.

When Cain was expelled from the Garden of Eden, God put a mark upon him, that all other persons would recognize him and not kill him.

The best of my research indicates it seems to have been a mark of red. (Red skin on the forehead or something similar.) Cain looked different from all the other people.

God gave Cain and his descendants almost a thousand years to repent and serve Him. But they did not repent. (They are not the sons of God.)

These Nephilim were the results of "the sons of God" mingling, and mixing with the beautiful "daughters of men." This produced a race of violent, and insolent giants or *gibborim*.

Cain's daughters were the daughters of men. This race of people can be found on map #1, as being on the east side of the Tigris River, to the northeast.

3874 B.C. Adam and Eve had Seth, a son in Adam's

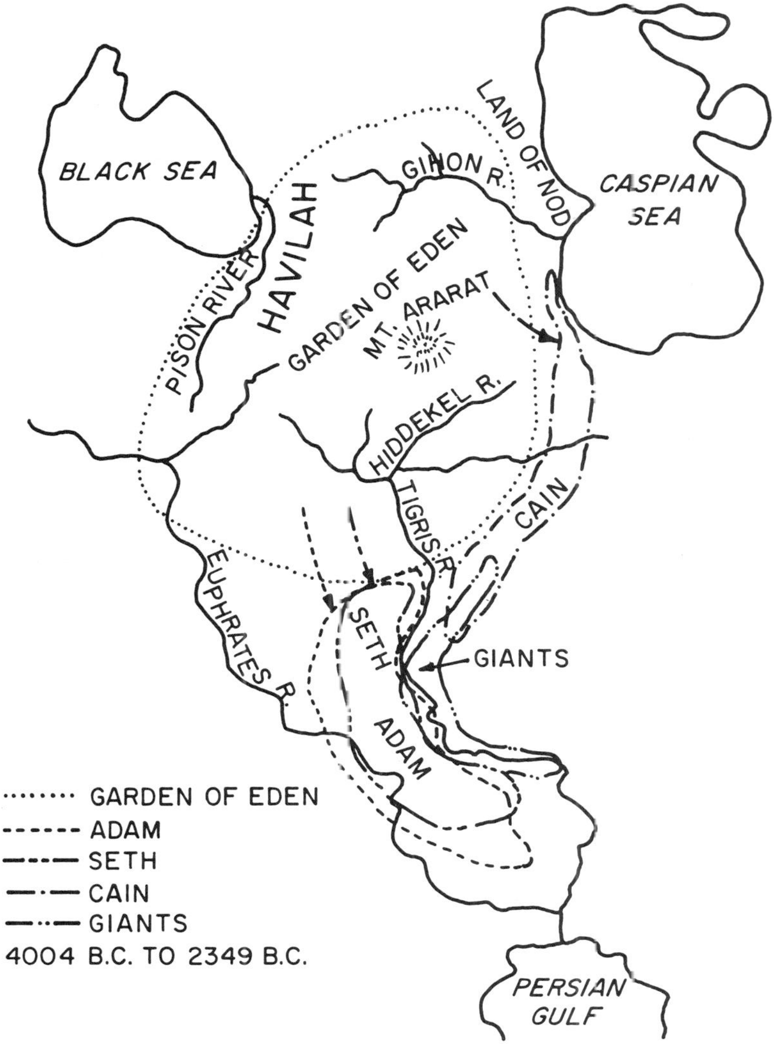

BLACK SEA
CASPIAN SEA
LAND OF NOD
GIHON R.
HAVILAH
PISON RIVER
GARDEN OF EDEN
MT. ARARAT
HIDDEKEL R.
TIGRIS R.
CAIN
EUPHRATES R.
SETH
GIANTS
ADAM
PERSIAN GULF
GARDEN OF EDEN
ADAM
SETH
CAIN
GIANTS
4004 B.C. TO 2349 B.C.

Map 1

own image. The descendants of Adam and Seth were the "sons of God." Because they worshipped God, and kept His commandments, with love and honor. Genesis 4:25: And Adam knew his wife again, and she bare a son, and called his name Seth, for God said she, hath appointed me another seed instead of Abel, whom Cain slew. And to Seth, to him also there was born a son; and he called his name Enos: then began men to call upon the name of the Lord.

This group (race) of people left the area of Eden, and filtered down between the Euphrates River, and the Tigris River.

Now we have two races of people. The Tigris River between them. Cain on the east and Adam and Seth on the west. "The daughters of men," and "the sons of God."

As these two races of people traded their products back and forth, they came in contact with each other occasionally and began to mix.

God being dissatisfied with mankind, marked their offspring by confusing their chromosomes. The results were, their stature was very abnormal. They were so very much larger than the normal people, they were freaks (giants).

This was a mark against the "sons of God" for breaking the laws of God. The undefiled with the defiled. Some of the earliest records show the giants were superhuman in size, and in strength. With the giants ranging between nine feet and fifteen feet tall, you can see how they would tower above the Semitic people of this age, who were small people, ranging from five feet to five feet five inches.

You can get a picture of this fearsome race of giants. These first giants do not seem to be as fierce as the later giants in the second and third groups, who were men of war and very evil, and very cruel.

Men continually sinned before God daily. At this

point God repented that he had ever made man.

After Adam, came his son Seth, his son Enos, his son, Cainan, his son Mahalaleel, his son Jared, his son Enoch, his son Methuselah, his son Lamech, his son Noah and his sons Shem, Ham and Japheth (2448 B.C.).

God told Noah to build the ark. In Genesis 6:14: Make thee an ark of gopher wood. Men were so evil in their hearts, God was compelled to punish them. God cannot tolerate sin. "He hates it." And brings judgment against it.

The first giants of 2469 B.C. and their descendants were drowned in the Flood; God sent the Flood in 2349 B.C. All of Cain's descendants drowned, along with all of Adam's, except eight persons.

God spared only Noah, Shem, Ham and Japhet, and their wives. Eight (8) persons, survived to replenish the earth with godly, holy, clean people, as Adam had been at creation.

Noah and his sons, and their wives started anew 2348 B.C. into a clean earth.

Check map #1 for site for the area, where these people dwelt in the old world.

Did you notice Cain named his sons names that were to honor God in their meanings. Which God did not accept. Because of the rebellion against God and Cain refused to repent.

Seth named his sons similar or the same names Cain used for his sons. God did accept Seth's sons and blessed them. Using Noah to replenish the earth's population after the destruction and purging by the waters of the flood.

It sets a pattern of evil trying to copy the good; all through the Bible. Even in the New Testament. The Nephilim were on the earth between 4000 B.C. and the time of the flood 2349 B.C.

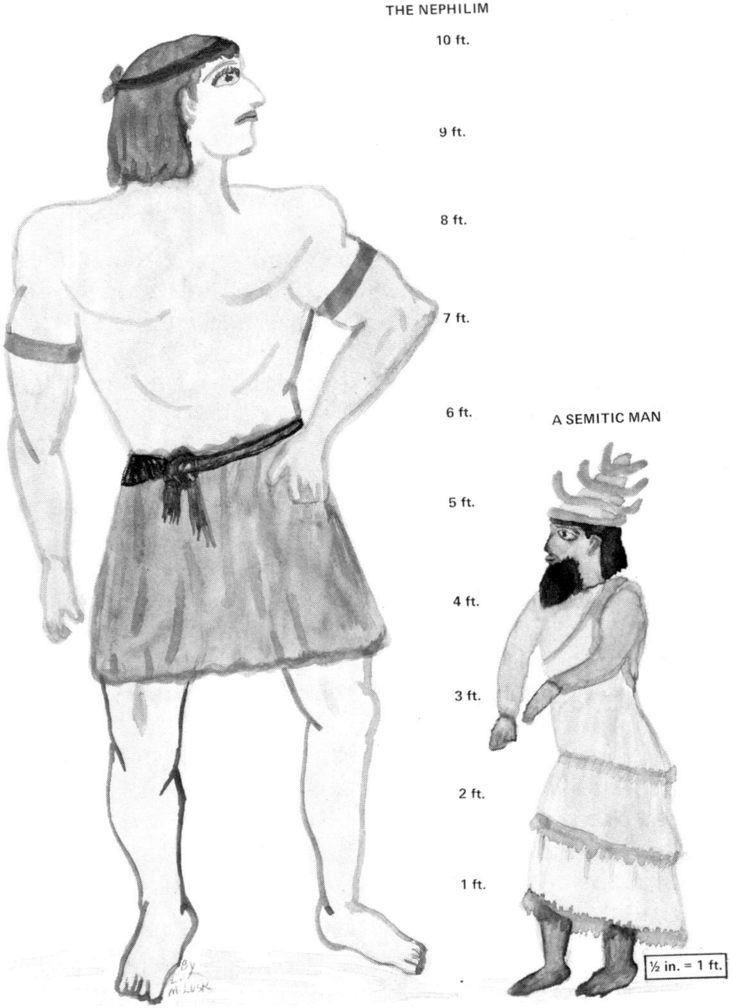

Fig. 1 The Nephilim

CHAPTER THREE

The Rephaim

After the Flood, giants were called Rephaim and Rapha. (2348 B.C.) Noah came out of the ark, with his family of three sons, their wives and his own wife. The animals also came forth from the ark.

The mountain Ararat was so high, and the sides were so steep, and rocky; they had to descend to the low lands.

The rivers Euphrates and Tigris furnished plenty of water and the land was fertile. Here Noah planted his vineyards. They also raised other food crops. (Noah had the grape plants and seed in the ark with him and the animals for their food all the time they were shut up.)

2347 B.C. Genesis 9:20: And Noah began to be a husbandman, and he planted a vineyard). Verse 21: (And he drank of the wine and was drunken; and he was uncovered within his tent. Verse 22: And Ham, the father of Canaan saw the nakedness of his Father, and told his brothers without. Verse 24: And Noah awoke from his wine and knew what his younger son had done unto him. Verse 25: And he said cursed be Canaan; a servant of servants shall be unto his brethren. All their relations, uncles, nephews, brothers, and cousins were all called brethren.

My theory is God caused Ham to have a mark, causing him and his descendants to be different, from all the other people. It is the same pattern that God caused to come to Cain. . .except his mark was red, and Ham's was black.

His son Cush and his sons were the people who developed Africa and Ethiopia.

Some of the giants to follow in this age were black. So we see the first giants to appear after the Flood were from Ham. God included in the curse a disturbance of the genes and chromosomes. The same he did to Cain's offspring. These people were sinful by nature.

Shem also had descendants who were sinful people and they were mixing with Egyptians and other ungodly nations, causing some of his descendants to become giants also. His giant offspring were brown.

This is the second group of giants from creation. The third group of giants came at a later date; through the tribe of Benjamin.

Some of these second groups of giants were called Nubian. These were Negroid from the Anglo and Egyptians in Sudan, between the Red Sea and Egypt. They were slaves in Egypt. They were kept by the pharaohs and kings of many countries because they were oddities.

The Rephaim were probably an aboriginal people of which the Emin and Anakim and Zuzim were branches. (We discuss these groups later.)

This second group of giants are found in the land of Canaan 2218 B.C. Genesis 10:15: And Canaan, begat Sidon, his first born and Heth. Verse 16: And the Jebusites, and the Amorites, and the Girgasites. Verse 17: And the Hivites and the Arkite and the Sinite. Verse 18: And the Ardvadite and the Zemorite, and the Hamathite: and afterwards were the families of Canaanites spread abroad.

These are the people cursed by Noah, back in 2347

B.C., because of Ham's sinful act. As these people began to spread over the country along the coast line of the Mediterranean Sea, and over to the Jordan River, they began to fall further from the original worship of God, as taught to them by their forefathers. They were becoming more sinful every day. Going their own ways. They were now beginning to worship idols. They traveled as far as Egypt and settled there. In this age Egyptians living in Egypt were called Hamites, or the Land of Ham. Psalms 105:23: Israel also came into Egypt; and Jacob sojourned in the land of Ham.

There were giants scattered from the land of Shinar (Babylon) to Egypt. Also South to the Dead Sea, at Mount Seir. Even on the east side of Jordan.

After God confounded the people's speech at Babel, they became four races: red, yellow, black, and white. They had become so numerous, and evil, God again confused the genes and chromosomes of the holy men mixing with the unholy women. Again giants were born, reappearing over the land. This second group we will place between 2347 B.C. and about 1700 B.C.

From Ham we have Seir's son Hori. The Horites came from Hori. Sometimes they were called Horim. Giants were living in Mount Seir before the time of Abraham. The Horites were cave dwellers in 1917 B.C.

The Zuzim lived in the land of Ham 1917 B.C. A primitive race of giants. Ham is an area between the Red Sea and Egypt, east of the Jordan River.

The Zuzim were the same people as the Zamzummin, who inhabited the land of the Ammonites, but were finally killed by the Ammonites.

The Philistines were also descendants of Ham. Their ancesters were Paehrusene and Casluham. Giants were among these Philistines also.

In 1921 B.C. Abram left the land of the Chaldea to go to Canaan. Because of the famine in the land he journeyed on to Egypt, in 1920 B.C.

Remember Lot his nephew was with Abram. The famine eased and after two years food was plentiful again in Canaan, in about 1918 B.C.

Abram's people and animals were of such a great number, and Lot's people and animals had multiplied to great numbers. It was becoming quite a problem for them all to remain together, because of the watering of the animals and feeding them, so they separated. 1917 B.C., Lot chose to live in the plains of Jordan. Toward Sodom and Gomorrah. Abram dwelled in the land of Canaan. But the land was wicked. (The people of the land.) Abram moved to the plain of Mamre in Hebron.

1910 B.C., Abram's son Ishmael was born of an Egyptian mother. From this union came a brown race of people, who lived in the desert. At this point, 1898 B.C., the angels visited Abram and told him, "Sarah would bear him a son (Isaac)." At this time Abram moved South to Kadesh and Shur, and Gerar.

Let us go back and have a look at Lot in 1987 B.C. He had left Sodom and Gomorrah. He went to live in the mountains east of these cities, when God destroyed Sodom and Gomorrah.

Lot's wife was turned into a pillar of salt, (as they fled to the mountains), when she looked back. The daughters of Lot agreed to each bear a child from their father so his name, and seed would not die out. Lot's oldest daughter got her father drunk and lay with him. . .she bore him a son. He was named Moab, who was the father of the Moabites. This happening was a sinful act against the law of God. God did not approve of it.

These Moabites were a very tall people, or they could be called giants. It's a known fact even today if a person is over seven feet tall he is considered to be a giant.

In 1986 B.C. Lot's second daughter bore him a son too. Following the acts and urging of her older sister.

He was named Ben-Ammi. He was the father of the children of Ammon, or sometimes calles the Ammonites.

In 1897 B.C. Sarah bore Abram the son, who had been promised of God. He was named Isaac. Abram was one hundred years old and Sarah about ninety years old when Isaac was born. Sarah drove Hagar and her son Ishmael out into the desert, where they dwelt in the wilderness of Paran. God blessed them. God made a nation of Ishmael. He later took a wife from his mother's people, the Egyptians.

1872 B.C., Abram named a well of water, and the area also the same name, Beer-Sheba. This same year God tempts Abram to offer his son Isaac as a burnt offering to God. Sarah died 1860 B.C. Abraham bought land and buried her in the land of Heth.

These people are mentioned to show the time setting, and who their descendants were. In a later chapter we will see giants coming from some of these people.

Back to 1913 B.C. The Bible tells us the giants were attacked, along with the normal people whom they lived among, in a great drive by Chedorlaomer the King of Elam, (east of Babylon), and his armies. Genesis 14:5: And in the fourteenth year, came Chedorlaomer and the kings that were (allies) with him and smote the Rephaim (giants) in Ashteroth, Karmin and the Zumin in Ham, and the Emin in Shaveh Kiriathaim. Verse 6: And the Horites in their Mount Seir, unto Elparah which is by the wilderness. Verse 7: And they returned and came to the Enmishpat, which is Kadesh and smote all the Amalekites and also the Amorites that dwelt in Hazezonamar.

As we read this setting of scripture we see there were giants here 1915 B.C. The Emin were called terrible men, because of their fierce aspect. They were aboriginal inhabitants of Mount Seir. They were cave dwellers. The Emin are the same tribe or clan of people as the Horites, another name for the Horites were the Hivites, who lived North of Gibeon. These people were very wicked. They were idol worshipers.

Cherdorlaomer made several drives in different years to attack these ancient peoples. He made them pay him tribute. He will be mentioned again later. His allies were Amorophel, King of Shinar, Ariach, King of Ellasar, and Tidal, King of Nations, Geiim.

We have had several groups of giants in this chapter. There are no records of any of the giants ever being God fearing, holy men. They are always described as a fierce, warlike group of people. They have appeared as a curse God put on their ancestors. They were very abnormal. If you noticed they lived among ungodly, idol worshiping people. You can find them and the tribes of people they lived with on map #2.

All the groups of giants mentioned in the chapter did not dwell at the same place. They all did not live at the exact same time. As you locate them in different areas on map #2, you can see where they have been mentioned to have lived, in the Bible scriptures.

How many of them that were at each geographic setting at one time is unknown. They were scattered over quite a large area, between 2348 B.C. and 1915 B.C.

Some of the Rephaim were great people, powerful, and an advanced civilization. They lived in the early bronze age, therefore some of their weapons and shields were made of bronze.

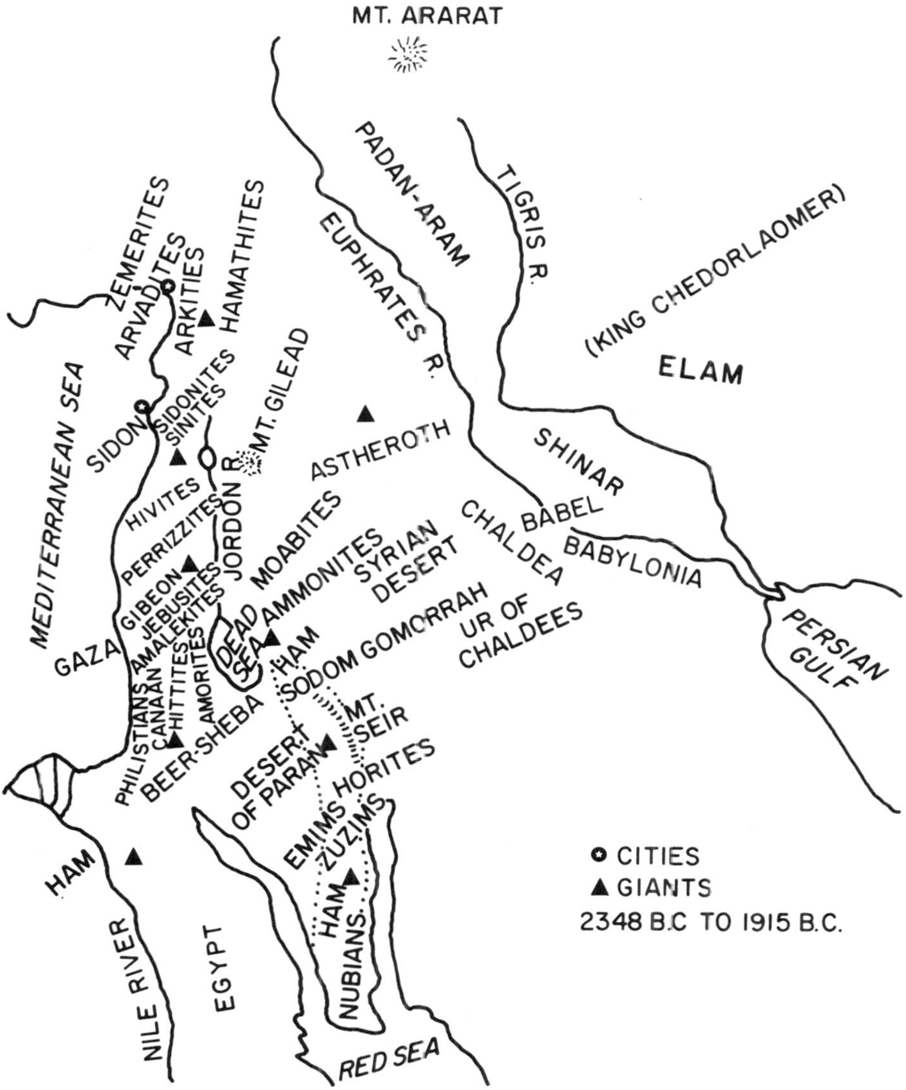
MT. ARARAT
PADAN-ARAM
TIGRIS R.
(KING CHEDORLAOMER)
ELAM
EUPHRATES R.
ZEMERITES
ARVADITES
ARKITIES
HAMATHITES
MEDITERRANEAN SEA
SIDONITES
SINITES
MT. GILEAD
SIDON
JORDON R.
ASTHEROTH
SHINAR
HIVITES
PERRIZZITES
MOABITES
BABEL
CHALDEA
BABYLONIA
SYRIAN
DESERT
AMMONITES
GIBEON
JEBUSITES
AMALEKITES
DEAD SEA
GAZA
HAM
SODOM GOMORRAH
UR OF
CHALDEES
PERSIAN
GULF
HITTITES
AMORITES
CANAAN
PHILISTIANS
BEER-SHEBA
MT.
SEIR
DESERT
OF PARAN
HORITES
EMIMS
ZUZIMS
HAM
NILE RIVER
EGYPT
HAM
NUBIANS.
RED SEA
CITIES
GIANTS
2348 B.C TO 1915 B.C.

Map 2

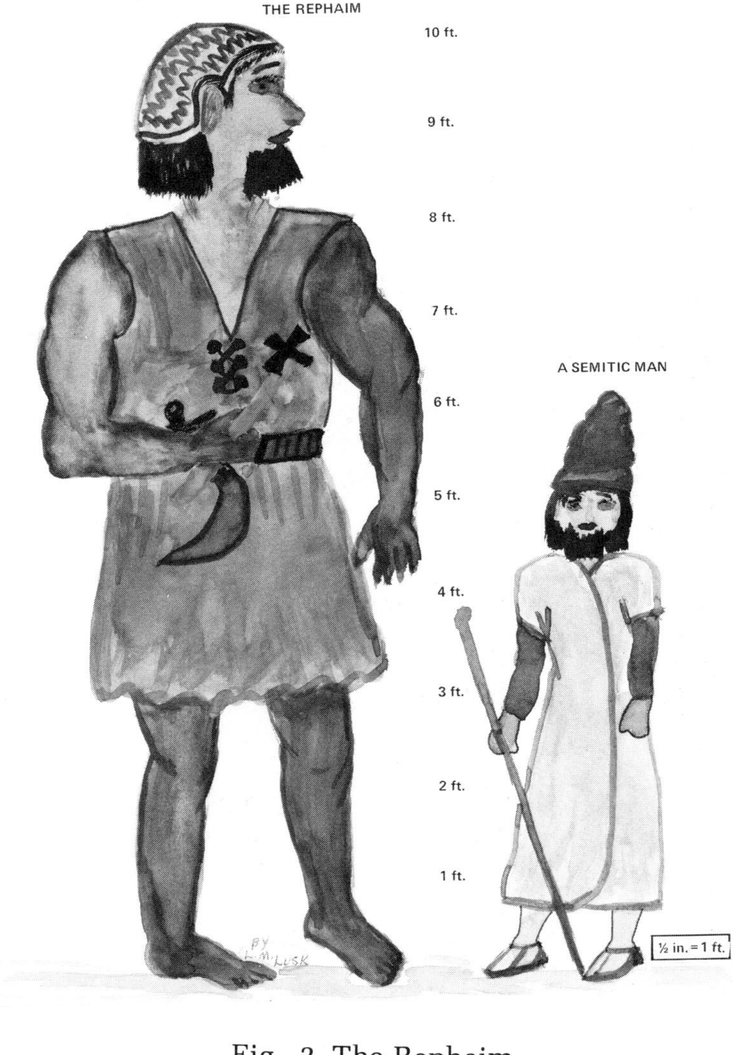

Fig. 2 The Rephaim

CHAPTER FOUR

The Giants After Abraham's Time

There was a fragment of the former giants in the land. In this chapter we are talking about another group of giants, than has been discussed in the previous chapters.

In 2056 B.C. Abram left the Land of Canaan and went to the plain of Moreh. The Bible tells us it was because of the wickedness of the people, in the Land of Canaan.

1920 B.C., he traveled south to Bethen and Hai, south, continuing on into Egypt. After two years, in 1918 B.C., he moved into the plain of Mamre in Hebron. In 1917 B.C. he and his people fought the giants in Paran. These probably were the Zuzim and Emmin. These people were early citizens of Moag.

About 1913 B.C, the Lord made a covenant with Abram. Gen. 15:18: Saying, unto thy seed have I given this land, from the river of Egypt unto the great river Euphrates. Verse 19: The Kenites, and the Kenizzites and the Kadonites. Verse 20: And the Hitties and the Perizzites and the Rephaim (giants. Verse 21: And the Amorites and the Canaanites and the Girgashites, and the Jebusites. Notice in verse 20 the Lord told Abram he would have the land that the giants owned at that time.

Also later on we shall see, one giant by name is called an Amorite.

Sarai gave her maid Hagar the Eygptian to be wife unto Abram. Afterwards in the process of the time of nature, Hagar bore Abram a son. Abram named him Ishmael. God had promised Abram and Sarai a son. But as humans become impatient, they try and help God out. Sarai wanted a son of her own since she was getting old and God had not given them the son he had promised. Abram was already ninety years old. Of course things didn't work out for any good, for any of them. Hagar turned on her mistress and taunted her saying "I have a son from Abram and you don't have a son."

Sarai became so tired of the taunting, she drove Hagar and her son Ishmael out into the desert. Abram was very sad, but God told him to let them go as Sarai had commanded them. God told Abram he would bless Ishmael and make a great nation of him. Abram lived in Beer-Sheba at this time. God wanted the child he would give Abram and Sarai to be the forerunner of the Israelites, his people. (The twelve tribes of Jews.) This came about through Abram's son Isaac. Jesus also came from this lineage.

God made another covenant with Abram, concerning Isaac, in 1889 B.C. Genesis 17:5: Neither shall thy name be Abram any more, but thy name shall be Abraham, for a father of many nations have I made thee. Verse 10: This is my covenant, which ye shall keep, between me and you and thy seed after thee; every man child among you shall be circumcised. Verse 14: And the uncircumcised man child whose flesh of his foreskin is not circumcised, that soul shall be cut off from his people; he hath broken my covenant.

Abraham circumcised Ishmael that day and Ishmael was thirteen years old. (Of course this took place before Hagar and Ishmael were driven out into the desert.)

Isaac was born 1898 B.C. and Abraham circumcised him on the eighth day, as the covenant with God.

The reason these people are being mentioned is to show there were giants from the lineage of Isaac, down through Esau and Jacob.

In 1860 B.C. God had told Abraham not to mix with the ungodly people of the country he traveled through.

God had sent his messengers, angels, to tell him he would have a son yet. All the fulfillment of the promise had not been granted. (That the lands would be given to his seed.)

In 1857 B.C. Abraham pledged for a wife for Isaac, not to be taken from the Canaanites. He sent his servant to the land of Mesopotamia, to the city of Nahor to look for a wife for Isaac. This is the same country Abraham and Sarah came from.

These people were not as advanced as the Canaanites were, and not nearly so wicked. The servant found the niece of Sarah, Rebekah by name. After making a pledge with her father, he took her back to become a wife to Isaac.

Rebekah was barren, she bore Isaac no son (or children). Isaac entreated the Lord for his wife. The Lord answered with a double portion blessing, by giving Rebekah twin sons.

The older twin was named Esau (red and hairy). The younger twin was named Jacob. Isaac loved Esau best and Rebekah loved Jacob best. From Esau came the Arab people. He had twelve sons who were called Dukes. From Jacob came the twelve tribes of the Jews. He also had twelve sons.

As we view these two tribes of people even today, they are still warring between themselves, as their fathers fought for the birthright (the blessing from their father and from God, over all else). Today they are warring over the land. As this double portion blessing divided and the brothers became estranged from each other, we too receive great blessings and allow them to become a very great conflict to us and to others.

In 1853 B.C., Esau married the daughter of one of the chieftains of Edom, (Edomites), which were also called Hivites. These people were ungodly. Abraham and Sarah were very sad about Esau's marriage to this forbidden wife (forbidden by God).

The Horites lived as far north as Gibeon and Shechem in the time of Esau's and Jacob's sons. The Horites are now (at this time,) commonly thought to be Hurrians of Media. The Hittites also advanced to this area. They came from a southern area; some passed on through, but some settled down and stayed. The nobles of these groups were called Aryans. The peasants were perhaps Armenoids, they were servants unto the Aryans. Some Hivites also lived near Palestine.

Esau also married two other wives of the forbidden Canaanites. Genesis 36:2: Esau took his wives of the daughters of Canaan, Adah, the daughter of Elon the Hittite, and Ahalibamah, the daughter of Ziebon the Hivite. Verse 8: Thus dwelt Esau in Mount Seir Esau is Edom. Verse 12: And Timma was concubine to Eliphaz, Esau's son, and she bore to Eliphaz Amalek. Now we see giants over the land again.

One of Esau's grandsons was named Seir. There also was a mountain named Seir. A son of Seir was Hori, (Horim), the Horites were from this man Hori.

There was a stronghold of giants at Mount Seir. These giants were cave dwellers. They also were war-like people.

(1796 B.C.) Why were the descendants of Esau giants? Because he went out among the forbidden un-godly people and took wives, which was a dishonor to God and to Abraham and Isaac.

God confused the genes and chromosomes and the giants were born. Later these ungodly people fought against the holy men of God, who passed through their land, under the leadership of Moses, when he led the captives out of Egypt.

Seems like some people just desire to be wicked, and break the laws of God. Esau surely had a godly father and mother. Even the angels of God visited them on several occasions. Yet Esau followed after wickedness and took pleasures in the forbidden things. Surely he did hate his birthright. It was better at the hands and will of Jacob, the smaller and weaker brother.

1780 B.C. Esau's name was changed to Edom (red). So we see the Arabians, who are truly red men. (1740 B.C.) Here are the names of the sons of Esau: Eliphaz. Reuel, Jeush, Jaalam and Korah. Some of his grandsons were fathers of giants. Seir has already been mentioned; others are Hori, Bela, Amalek, Dishon, Uz and Aran, whose descendants were Horites. These sons and their sons were becoming very numerous until about the year 1676 B.C.

1752 B.C., Jacob went to a far country in the east, because he was afraid of Esau, and what he might do to him because he stole his birthright. Actually he went to Mesopotamia and worked for his uncle (Rebekah's brother, Laban). While he was there he acquired two wives, both sisters, Leah and Rachel.

(1750 B.C.) The sons born to Jacob and Leah were Reuben, Simeon, Levi, Judah and Issachar. His concubine Bilah had sons for him named Dan and Naphtali. His concubine Zilpah had sons of Jacob named Gad and Asher. Rachel his second wife bore him two sons Joseph and Benjamin in 1729 B.C.

In 1729 B.C., Jacob lived in the Land of Canaan. Joseph's older brothers sold him into slavery to a band of Midianite traders. God watched over Joseph and blessed him. 1720 B.C., Joseph explained some dreams of the Pharaoh. Again in 1718 B.C., Joseph explained more of the dreams of the Pharaoh. Joseph was given a wife whose name was Asenath. Afterwards the Pharaoh put Joseph in charge of all the food in Egypt. In 1711 B.C., Joseph had two sons in Egypt, their names were Manasseh and Ephraim.

In the year 1708 B.C., a very severe famine hit the land of Canaan. Jacob, who was called Israel, and all his sons and their large families, servants and animals were without food. (All the eleven sons except Joseph.) 1707 B.C., Jacob sent some of his sons into Egypt to buy food. Not knowing Joseph his beloved son was ruler over all the food in Egypt. (His wicked brothers had told their father a wild beast had killed Joseph many years back.) Before revealing himself, Joseph asked for Benjamin his younger brother to be brought to him. Benjamin was at least twenty-two years old at this time.

The sons of Benjamin were Belah, Becher, Ashbel, Gera, Naaman, Ehi, Rosh, Muppim, Huppin, and Ard. Take note of the son Belah, he is the father of Rephaim, the giants in a following chapter. This is why we have gone into the lineage and dates of the people, descendants of Jacob, in this chapter.

In this chapter we laid the groundwork for the coming chapter, when we begin to name the last group of giants by their names. We must keep in mind they were just men, abnormal because of sin in the lives of their ancestors, and it followed down into their lives also.

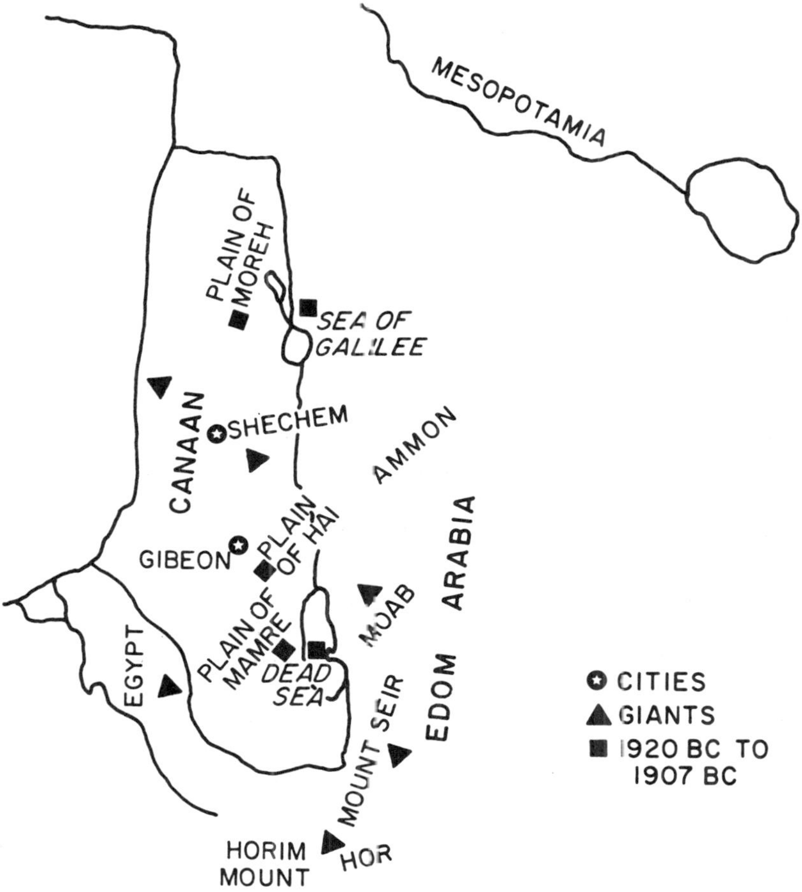
MESOPOTAMIA
PLAIN OF MOREH
SEA OF GALILEE
CANAAN
SHECHEM
AMMON
GIBEON
PLAIN OF HAI
ARABIA
PLAIN OF MAMRE
MOAB
DEAD SEA
EGYPT
MOUNT SEIR
EDOM
HORIM
MOUNT
HOR
CITIES
GIANTS
1920 BC TO
1907 BC

Map 3

CHAPTER FIVE

The Giant Named Anak

In 1490 B.C. there was a giant named Anak, his father's name was Araba. There also was a city named after Arba. Joshua 14:15: (And the name of Hebron before was Kirjatharba, which Arba was a great man among the Anakim. And the land had rest from war). Caleb had kept the faith and courage to trust God. He was rewarded, by an inheritance in the land of promise, occupied by some giants, the Anakim.

Moses had sent spies into the Land of Canaan to see if the children of Israel (whom Moses was leading to the land of promise), could take the land from its present inhabitants. Numbers 13:22: And they ascended the south and came into Hebron, where Ahiman, Sheshia and Talmia, the children of Anak were.

Hebron was sometimes referred to as the city of the four, Anak and his three giant sons. The spies returned and said, no, we cannot take this land, because of the giants living in the country.

Fruits of the land were brought back, to show Moses what the land produced. One cluster of grapes was so huge, two men carried it upon a pole across their shoulders. Pomegranates and figs were also proof of the abundance of the richness of the land. As God had told his people, he would lead them to a land of milk and honey, Canaan was that land and very rich as God promised.

Numbers 13:28: Nevertheless the people be strong that dwell in the land, and the cities are walled, and very great, and moreover we saw the children of Anak there. Verse 32: And they brought up an evil report of the land which they had searched, unto the children of Israel saying, the land through which we have gone to search, it is a land that eateth up the inhabitants thereof; and all the people that we saw in it are men of a giant stature. Verse 33: And there we saw the giants, the sons of Anak which come of the giants, and we were as grasshoppers in their sight.

Here we find Arba, his son Anak, his sons Ahiman, Sheshia, and Talmai, and their offspring. They lived in the city of Hebron. These giants are descendants of Arphaxad, sons called Sala (or Shelah) in I Chronicles 1:18. (Arahaxad is the third son of Shem.)

Anak was the father of the Anakim. There also is some information, that the Anakim lived in Palestine about this age. They were a powerful people.

The true faithful spies that came back with a good report were the leaders Caleb and Joshua. They had faith that God would help them take the land for the Israelites. But the people were afraid, they turned south into the desert, where they wandered for forty years. God punished the men who doubted God's strength. They all died as they wandered around. Their children were allowed to enter the promised land under the leadership of Joshua. However, they still had to fight these giants and kill them, at a later date.

About this time there were also giants in the land of Caphtor. These are the descendants of Ham. Caphtor was later called Egypt. These giants were called Caphtorim.

Goshen is a city in the land of Rahab also called

the Land of Ham. It was from the city or land of Goshen the Israelites were led by Moses on their long trek to the land of Canaan.

1490 B.C., these Anakim were also called Zuzim and Emim. They were the same race of people, called by a different name in different parts of the country or land. These two groups lived in Moab.

In Deuteronomy 2:10: The Emim dwelt there in these times past, a people great and many as tall as the Anakim. Verse 11: Which also were accounted giants, as the Anakim; but the Moabites called them Emim. Verse 20: That also was accounted a land of giants. Giants dwelt therein in old times, and the Ammonites called them Zamzammin.

Moab and Ammon were the sons of Lot. As Moses led the Israelites through their land, the Lord would not allow them to take that land. They were commanded not to destroy anything, crops, land, animals or people. God had given this land to Lot.

These verses are given to prove that in the Bible these tribes of giants were all Anakim. The time is about fifty years later than it was thought that these giants had all been killed off by God, in the Land of Moab. (The three sons of Anak are still living in Hebron, across the Jordan River.) David and his men drove them out later. God had destroyed these above-mentioned giants so Moses could lead the Israelites through this country. However, they were confronted with the Moabites and the Ammonites as they passed.

Some of the old-time giants God had destroyed in this area were the Horim, Avim and the Caphtorim, as we have also mentioned the Zuzim and Emim.

1452 B.C., the Lord was with his people. They could have entered into Canaan when Moses sent the spies into the land. After forty years they did enter the promised land and still had the same battle to fight. It is said they entered this land through the back door.

Moses had died. Joshua and Caleb took the people onward to their destination.

Joshua 15:13: And unto Caleb the son of Jephrenneh he gave a part among the children of Judah, according to the commandment of the Lord to Joshua, even the city of Arba the father of Anak, which city is Hebron. Verse 14: And Caleb drove thence the three sons of Anak, Sheshia, Anihman and Talmia, the children of Anak. Also Joshua 21:11: And they gave them the city of Arba, the father of Anak, (which is the city Hebron) in the hill country of Judah, with its suburbs there go round about it.

Giants terrorized the Israelites entering Canaan until the time of David.

Gideon also fought and killed giants and took their land for an heritage as was promised him by the leaders.

So you can see the giants are being killed, and their races are beginning to vanish off the face of the earth.

Kish, the father of King Saul, also was a descendant of Arba.

As there was a great challenge to the Israelites, God's people, there is also a challenge for the Christians today to be faithful to our Lord. Some of our problems look as big as giants, but Christians should have no fear. We have the same God on our side as in the Bible times, who gave victory over giant problems, to those who trusted in him.

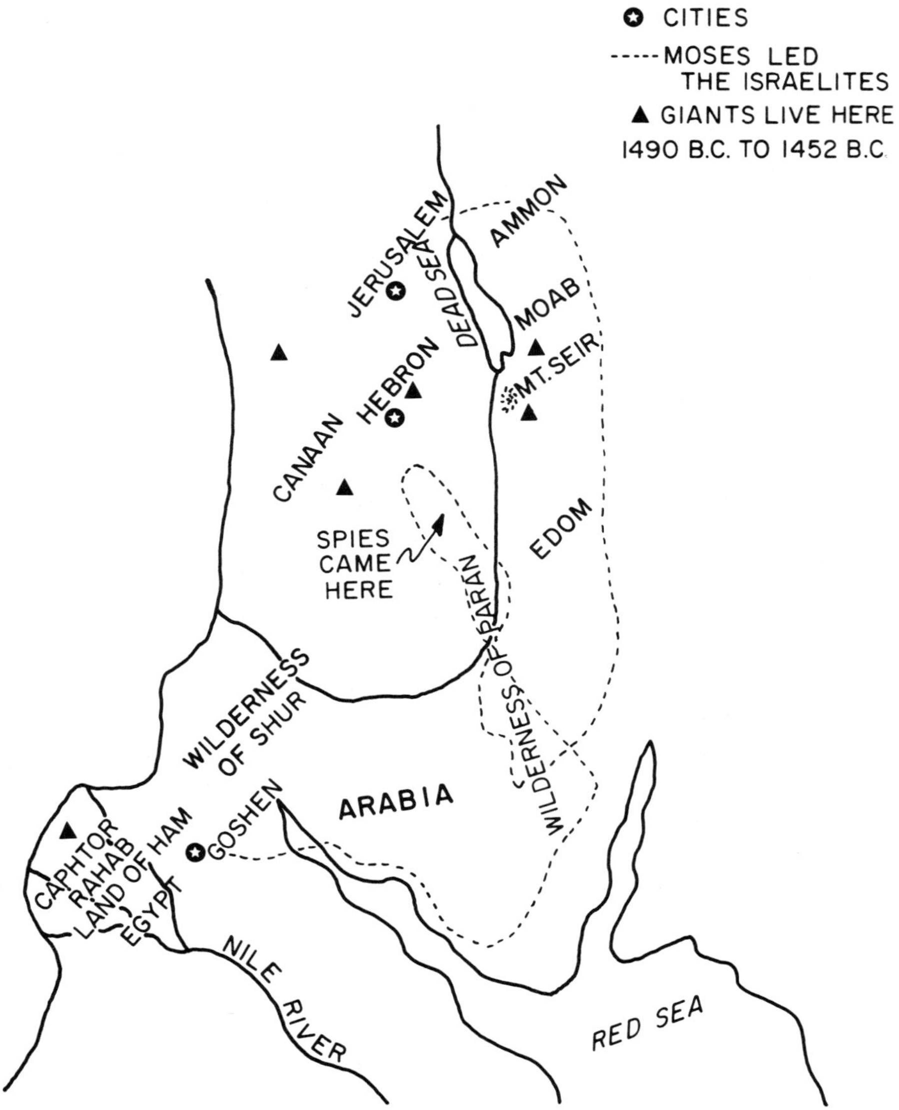
CITIES
MOSES LED THE ISRAELITES
GIANTS LIVE HERE
1490 B.C. TO 1452 B.C.
JERUSALEM
DEAD SEA
AMMON
MOAB
MT. SEIR
HEBRON
CANAAN
EDOM
SPIES CAME HERE
WILDERNESS OF PARAN
WILDERNESS OF SHUR
WILDERNESS
ARABIA
GOSHEN
CAPHTOR
RAHAB
LAND OF HAM
EGYPT
NILE RIVER
RED SEA

Map 4

CHAPTER SIX

The Giant King Og

1451 B.C. In King Og we see our first giant of royal prestige and ruling power. He is king over a very large kingdom, with great power. He seemed to rule the people very well. The land also prospered.

Prior to this chapter, the giants we have written about have been warriors in several combats. They have always been fighting on the side of the enemies of God's people.

King Og ruled over the land of Bashan. Bashan was a country between Syria and Arabia, with Canaan on the west side. The land was later divided into portions given to the twelve tribes of Israel. One portion to Reuben and a portion to Gad, and some to the half tribe of Manasseh (one of Joseph's sons).

The capital of Bashan was at Haran, just over the border into Syria. The Bible says in Deut. 3:1: Then we turned and went up the way to Bashan; and Og the King of Bashan came out against us, he and all his people to battle at Endrei.

You see the promised land was not just given to the Israelites, free and clear. They had to fight and drive the existing residents out of the land; so they could occupy it.

King Og lived among the Ammonites. The Ammonites were descendants of Lot's son Ammon. These people were a very wicked tribe. The Amorites are descendants of Canaan. The names sound similar. Deut. 3:3: So the Lord our God delivered into our hands Og also, the King of Bashan, and all his people; and we smote him until none was left to him remaining. Verse 4: And we took all his cities at that time, there was not a city which we took not from threescore cities, all the region of Argob, the kingdom of Og of Bashan.

Why would the land of Bashan be so desired by the Israelites? It was a land that grew the finest oak trees. Lumber was taken from them to make oars for the largest and greatest ships. Ezekiel 27:6: Of the oaks of Bashan have they made thine oars. (A) Verse 9: The ancients of Gebel and the wise men thereof were in thee thy caulkers; all the ships of the sea with their mariners were in thee to occupy thy merchandise. Lumber for ships, lumber for large columns (posts) in buildings.

Also famous for its cattle raised there. Amos 4:1: Hear this word, ye kine of Bashan that are in the mountains of Samaria, which oppress the poor, which crush the needy, which say to their masters, bring and let us drink. Deut. 32:14: Butter of kine and milk of sheep with fat of lambs, and rams of the breed of Bashan, and goats with the fat of kidneys of wheat: and thou didest drink the pure blood of the grapes. Listed in this verse we see a very large productive wealth. Kine (cows), sheep, goats and grapes and wheat. It appears people from adjoining countries came to Bashan to buy breeding stock of rams and bulls. Psalms 22:12: Many bulls have compassed me: strong bulls of Bashan have beset me. Also in Ezekiel 39:28: Ye shall eat the flesh of the mighty, and drink the blood of the princes of the earth, of rams, of lambs and of goats of bullocks, all of them fatlings of Bashan. In this verse the goats are considered, great goats. In these Bible verses we get a small glimpse of the great value of the products of

Bashan. We know they had iron in the land because later we mention, King Og's bedstead is made of iron. These people knew how to mine, smelt, and shape iron to make war articles such as spears, swords, knives, and some armor for protectiin in battle. There probably was gold and silver; brass had been used before iron, for war artifacts.

Actually Og was the one remnant of giants from the second group of giants, that we talked about from the date 2218 B.C. These earlier giants were Semites, kin to the Akkadians from 2475 B.C. They came down from Babel. The chief city they lived in was Aakad in the north from Bashan, into Ereck a southern district of Babylon or Syria. Some of these giants of old even ruled in some parts of Egypt, for a short time.

So you can see why Bashan was called the land of the giants. King Og was a very large giant. He was probably between twelve and fourteen feet tall. Some of the first and second groups were at least fifteen feet tall. Why do I assume he was this tall? In the Bible Deut. verse 3:11: For only Og King of Bashan remained of the remnants of giants; behold his bedstead was a bedstead of iron; is it not in Rabath of the children of Ammon? Nine cubits was the length thereof, and four cubits the breadth of it, after the cubit of a man. How much was a cubit? There were two versions, some called it twenty-one inches. Some called it eighteen inches. This is the version I have used to measure it. Thus nine cubits by eighteen inches gives us, thirteen feet and six inches long. Four cubits wide, four times eighteen inches gives us six feet wide. He was quite a man and warrior.

The later capital of Bashan was at Endrei. From this area King Og came against the children of God to do battle. He was a strong king and leader of his people. He fought well to retain his kingdom and protect his followers. He could not win, because he was an ungodly man. He had to yield all he had worked for and protected so long, to the children of God, because God was on their side. Joshua 13:12: All the kingdom of Og in Bashan, which reigned in Ashtaroth and in Endrei, who remained of the remnants of the giants. For these did Moses smite and cast them out. Also the Bible Amos verse 2:9: Yet destroyed I the Amorite before them, whose height was like the Cedars, and he was strong as the Oaks: yet I destroyed his fruit from above, and his roots from beneath. Even as God describes King Og he says he was one of the biggest and strongest of the giants.

In the Book of Psalms we see some verses that admonish the Israelites to give thanks to God, because he gave them victory over this great abnormal problem (giants). God took the land of Bashan from Og and gave it to them. These people loved God, had faith in his power, they worshiped him and kept his laws. (O give thanks for God's mercy.) Psalms 136:20: That God had killed him for the Israelites, King Og of Bashan. Aslo in Joshua 9:10: And all that he did to the kings of the Amorites, that were beyond Jordan, to Shion, King of Heshbon, and to Og, King of Bashan, which was at Ashtaroth. One more verse in Psalms 136:17: To him which smote great kings, for his mercy endureth forever. Verse 20: And Og the King of Bashan: for his mercy endureth forever. No wonder these people were full of praise to their God for his great mercy toward them.

At this point the great giants mentioned in the Bible have been killed and destroyed by the Israelites. 1450 B.C. the Lord also destroyed the Anakim. No giants were left in the land except at Gaza and Gath and Ashdod. Joshua 11:22: There was none of the Anakim left in the land of the children of Israel; only in Gaza, in Gath and in Ashdod there remained. These were three sons of Og. They were killed later by Joshua and Caleb. In the next chapter, they were in Philistia (the land of the Philistines).

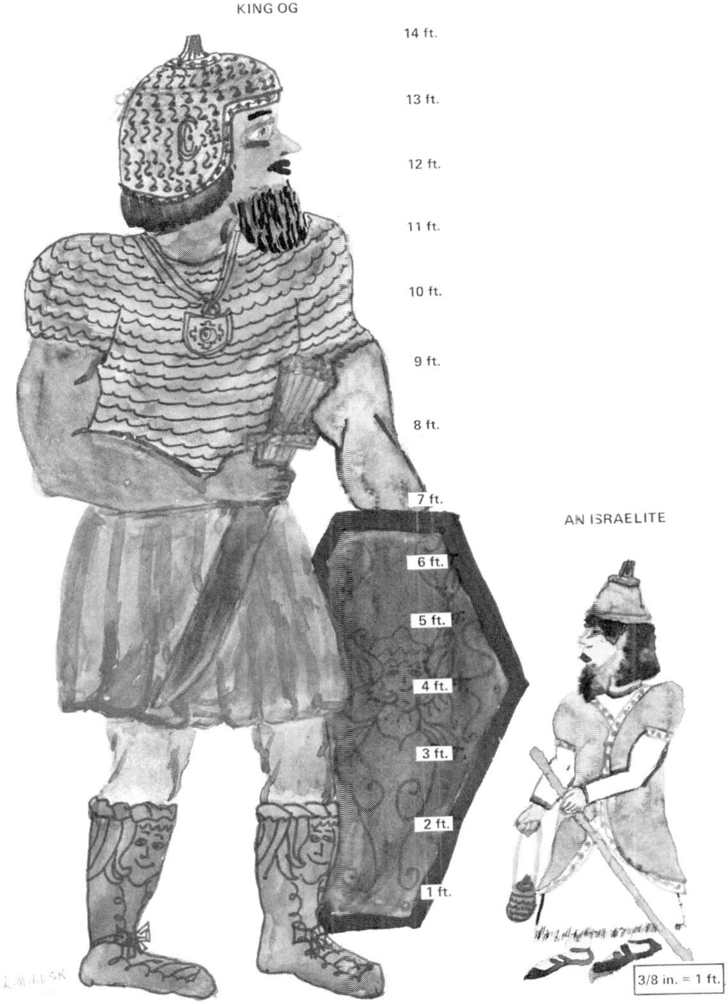

Fig. 3 The Giant King Og

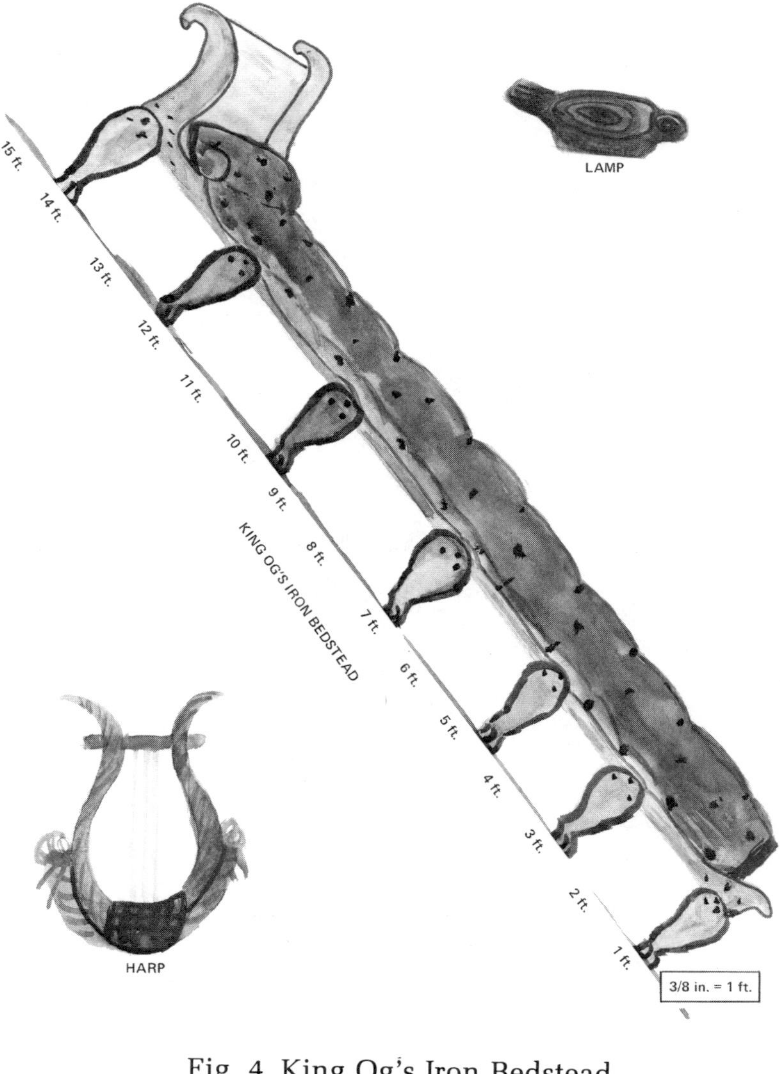

Fig. 4 King Og's Iron Bedstead

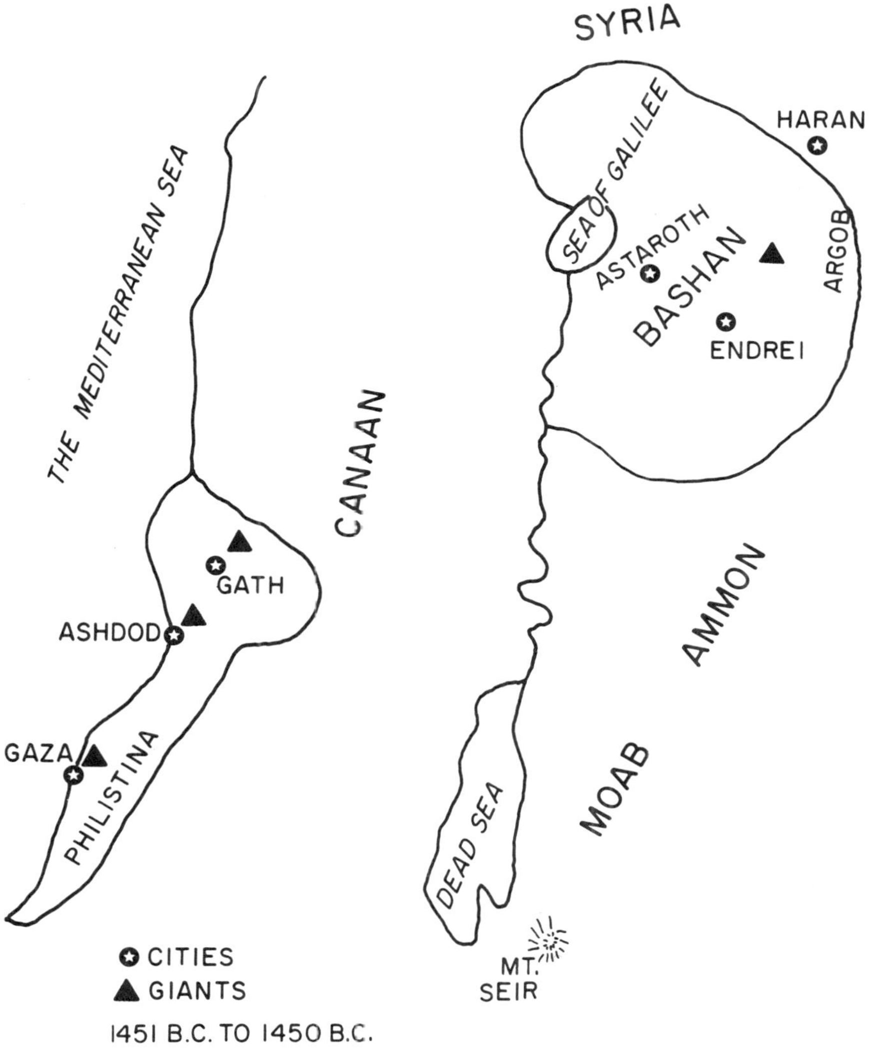
SYRIA
HARAN
SEA OF GALILEE
ASTAROTH
BASHAN
ARGOB
ENDREI
THE MEDITERRANEAN SEA
CANAAN
GATH
ASHDOD
AMMON
GAZA
PHILISTINA
MOAB
DEAD SEA
MT. SEIR
CITIES
GIANTS
1451 B.C. TO 1450 B.C.

Map 5

CHAPTER SEVEN

The Genealogy of the Third Group of Giants

(1444 B.C.) This time age is the last age of giants in Bible history. However, we must go back to 1932 B.C., the date of the birth of the father of these last giants. You may be surprised to read, these giants of the iron age were actually descendants of the sons of (Jacob) Israel. There were twelve sons born to Israel. They were Reuben, Simeon, Levi, Judah, Issachar, Zebulum, Dan, Joseph, Benjamin, Naphtali, Gad, and Asher. Our big question, which of the twelve sons did the giants come from? It was Benjamin. His sons were Bela, Ashlel, Ahorah, Noahn, and Rapha, (a giant).

Let us take a look at Bela for a little while. Bela had a son named Kish. Kish was the father of Saul. (Who became the king of Israel.) Saul had a son named Jonathan. Jonathan's son was Micah. 1400 B.C. Bela and his sons moved to Manaha. If you remember, when Saul was chosen by the Israelites to be their king, it was because he was head and shoulders taller than all the other men. So he must have been about six feet and five inches, even to near seven feet tall. He was almost a giant himself, but not quite.

Benjamin lived in the land of Canaan, with his father and brothers in 1729 B.C. Joseph had been sold into slavery, and was in Egypt in 1720 B.C. When Joseph was about thirty years old, the Pharaoh gave Joseph full power to rule over the food-stuff in Egypt. (He was made a ruler of the country.) In a dream God gave to Pharaoh a warning of a severe famine that would come to the land of Egypt. God's word is always true. The famine hit in 1708 B.C. Jacob and his sons, and their families, were without food in the land of Canaan. Joseph had stored several years of grain in Egypt. All the countries were sending people to buy corn and food from Egypt. In 1707 B.C., Jacob sent his sons to buy food in Egypt, not knowing Joseph was ruler over the storage. When they arrived Joseph pretended not to know who his brethren were. He asked for them to bring their brother Benjamin on the second trip or they could not have more food. Benjamin was already married and had sons of his own. After Joseph revealed himself, Jacob and all his sons moved to Egypt.

Since I have already listed Benjamin's sons, you can see the fifth son was Rapha. The Bible tells us this in I Chronicles 8:1: Now Benjamin begat Bela his firstborn, Ashbel the second and Aharah, the third. Verse 2: Nohan the fourth, and Rapha the fifth. It had been about 260 years from the time Benjamin moved to Egypt, that the record of his sons was recorded in 1444 B.C. The Bible tells us the heads of fathers lived in Ajalon. Some of Bela's offspring lived in Geba, and moved to Mamahath. Some went to Moab. Some lived in Gibeon and some near Jerusalem. In I Chronicles 8:40: And the sons of Ulam were mighty men of valor, archers, and had many sons, and son's sons, an hundred and fifty. All these are the sons of Benjamin. There were several generations of offspring. They lived in Jerusalem. I Chronicles 9:3: And in Jerusalem dwelt of the children of Judah, and of the children of Benjamin, and of the children of Ephraim, and Manasseh. Ephraim and Manasseh are the two sons of Joseph, each had one half tribe.

Rapha was born about 1406 B.C. The sons of Benjamin had married and mixed with the ungodly nations all around them, that God had forbidden them to marry. So the curse of God came upon them. Their genes and chromosomes were fouled up again; and we see giants from Benjamin. Rapha was a giant.

Giants were also called Rephaim in that day. This is the beginning of the third group of giants, upon the earth. It was also the last race of giants mentioned in the Bible.

These giants were south of Jerusalem, when the Israelites entered the country coming to the land of Canaan from Egypt. As Moses led the Israelites through the country of Moab, they came out to fight God's people. The descendants of Rapha were taking an ungodly stand against God's children, their Godly brethren.

Rapha was not only tall, but he was very strong of physique. Most giants were aggressive, warlike people. Both the second and the third groups were very hateful and aggressive. The first group (the Nephilim), before the Flood, did not seem to be so aggressive.

Remember back to chapter 6, we had three giant sons of King Og still living, at Gaza, Gath and Ashdod? As Moses led the Israelites through that country these giants were killed by Joshua, and Caleb. They also destroyed all the ungodly normal people with these giants. To clean the land of idol-worshipping people, before the children of God entered the land to dwell there.

This took place between 1450 B.C. and 1444 B.C. The third group of giants from Benjamin.

We will learn more about Rapha and sons of Rapha in the following chapter. We will recognize many of them by name. The famous Goliath being one of them.

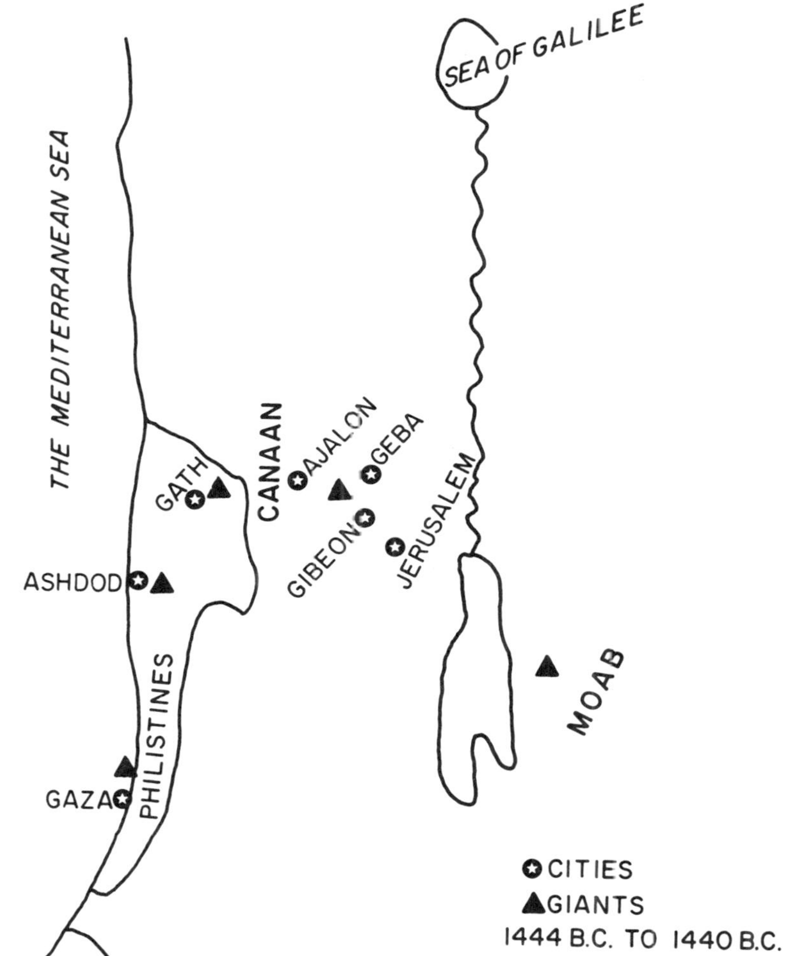
SEA OF GALILEE
THE MEDITERRANEAN SEA
CANAAN
AJALON
GEBA
GATH
JERUSALEM
GIBEON
ASHDOD
PHILISTINES
MOAB
GAZA
EGYPT
CITIES
GIANTS
1444 B.C. TO 1440 B.C.

Map 6

CHAPTER EIGHT

The Giant Rapha

1406 B.C., Rapha was born to Benjamin; he was the fifth and last son of Benjamin. Back in chapter 7, I mentioned some of Benjamin's sons were archers. In I Chronicles 10:1: Now the Philistines fought against Israel; and the men of Israel fled from before the Philistines and fell down slain (or wounded) in Mount Gilboa. Verse 3: And the battle went sore against Saul and the archers hit him and he was wounded of the archers. Verse 4: Then said Saul to his armorbearer, draw thy sword, and thrust me through therewith; lest these uncircumcised come and abuse me. But his armorbearer would not; for he was sore afraid. So Saul took a sword and fell upon it. (1200 B.C.) From these Bible verses we learn Rapha and his people are living with the Philistines. The Philistines were ungodly people. Although they were descendants of Abraham, they had not been circumcised, as God had commanded. God told Abraham to circumcise every male in his family and all his brethren. These uncircumcised people were idol worshipers, as were the Philistines they lived with, and married daughters of the Philistines.

By the year 1056 B.C. David and all of Israel

gathered together and went up against these wicked armies, and slew many of them, three hundred at one time.

The Canaanites also fought the Israelites. The Canaanites existed between 1800 B.C. and 1400 B.C. They were pre-Israelites and lived east of the Jordan River. There was also a group living on the west side of the Jordan River. They spoke the Semitic languages. Hebrew was one language spoken, especially by the godly people.

The ungodly people were Phoenicians, and Moabites. The Canaanites were Semitic stock. The Phoenicians, Amorites, and Canaanites, were from the third millennium, and lived in the northeast part of Arabia. They had come up under Egyptian control about 1500 B.C.

The Philistine people lived in the twelfth and thirteenth centuries. After being repulsed by Egypt about 1191 B.C. they invaded Canaan. Some of them had gone to Egypt from some of the islands in the ocean (Mediterranean Sea), probably the Greek Islands by later name. These came from the Hittite Empire. It was also in the iron age that they came to Canaan. The Philistines were non-Semitic, they were also uncircumcised in the time of David. There were giants living with each of these races of people just mentioned.

After Saul's death, God turned his kingdom over to David, the son of Jesse. In I Chronicles 11:15: Now three of the thirty captains went down to the rock to David into the cave of Adullam; and the host of the Philsitines encamped in the valley of Rephaim (giants). Verse 22: Benaiah, the sons of Jehoiada, the son of a valiant man of Kabzeel, who had done many acts; he slew two lionlike men of Moab. Verse 23: And he slew an Egyptian, a man of great stature, five cubits high (eight and one-half feet). And in the Egyptian's hand was a spear like a weaver's beam; and he went down to him with a staff, and plucked the spear out of the Egyptian's hand, and slew him with his own spear.

About one hundred and fifty years before this date some of the sons of Benjamin had moved to Moab. When the Israelites came marching through, under the leadership of Moses and Joshua, they came out against them and fought them. The Israelites slew 25,000 of the Benjaminites. They also slew their wives and children until there were only a few Benjaminites left.

The Benjaminites could not marry the daughters of Judah or any of the sons of Israel's daughters, because of a vow the men had made before God, because they were ungodly men (uncircumcised).

It looked as if the Benjaminites would die out, thus elimination of one whole tribe of the Israelites. The men of the tribe of Judah and his brethren, had a conference between themselves to avoid the loss of this one tribe. They worked out a plan to aid the Banjaminites and not break their vow, also assisting their brethren to acquire new wives to rebuild their tribe. The Israelites repented they had made the vow, but they could not break a vow between themselves and God.

After taking count of which tribes had come forth to join the battle with the Israelites, it was noted, none had come up from Jabeshgilead to join in the host of God's people. This tribe would have to be punished, for not responding to the call for help. (1406 B.C.) Judges 21:10: And the congregation sent thither twelve thousand men of the valiantest, and commanded them, saying, "Go and smite the inhabitants of Jabeshgilead with the edge of the sword, with the women and the children." Verse 11: And this is the thing that ye shall do, ye shall utterly destroy every male, and every woman that hath lain by man. Verse 12: And they found among the inhabitants of Jabeshgilead four hundred young virgins that had known no man by laying with any male, and they brought them unto the camp to Shiloh, which is in the land of Canaan. Verse 14: And Benjamin came again at that time; and they gave them wives which they had saved alive of the women of Jabeshgilead; and yet so they sufficed them not.

(1307 B.C).) Rapha was the father of the third and last group of giants. Their names were Saph (or Sippa), Ishabenob, Lahmi, and Goliath. So we see Rapha had four sons, these are the last giants recorded by the Bible. At this time we see David with his armies going out to battle against the ungodly, idol worshipping nations around Jerusalem. He or his warriors killed off these last giants. Let us look at a few Bible verses to prove these giants killed are the sons of Rapha.

(1033 B.C.) I Chronicles 20:1: And it came to pass that after the year was expired, at the time that kings go out to battle, Joab led forth the power of the army, and wasted the country of the children of Ammon, (Lot's son) and came and besieged Rabbah, but David tarried at Jerusalem, and Joab smote Rabbah, and destroyed it. Rabbah was a city in the land of the Ammonites. It was here these relations of King Og (giant) had kept his iron bedstead. I Chronicles 20:2: And David took the crown of their king from off his head, and found it to weigh a talent of gold, and there were precious stones in it. It was set upon David's head, and he brought also exceeding much spoil out of the city. A talent in Hebrew monetary value was worth $1,550.00 to $2,000.00.

(1018 B.C.) Verse 4: And it came to pass after this that there arose war at Gezer, with the Philistines; at which time Sebbechai the Hushathite slew Sippa (or Saph) that was of the children of the giant; and they were subdued. Verse 5: And there was war again with the Philistines, and Elhanan the son of Jair slew Lahmi the brother of Goliath the Gittite, whose spear-staff was like a weaver's beam. Verse 6: And yet again there was war at Gath, where was a man of great stature, whose fingers and toes were four and twenty, six on each hand and six on each foot, and he also was the son of the giant (Rapha). In this verse the son Ish-Benob is described. Verse 7: But when he defiled Israel, Jonathan the son of Shimea, David's brother slew him. Verse 8: These were born unto the giants in Gath; and they fell by the hand of David and by the hand of his servants.

In this chapter three of the four sons of Rapha have been killed, Sippa, Lohmi and Ish-Benob (the giant with twenty-four fingers and toes). There is still one son more to be disposed of, the famous giant Goliath; in the next chapter we will tell of this man.

In 2 Samuel 21:16: And Ish-Benob, which was of the giant (Rapha), the weight of whose spear weighed three hundred shekels of brass in weight, he being girded with a new sword, thought to have slain David. Verse 17: But Abishai, the son of Zeruiah succoured him, and smote the Philistine and killed him. In 1021 B.C., brass was used for war equipment before this time. In verse 16 we see the giant had a brass spear, but he had a new sword. Since iron had been introduced to the Philistines by this date, we assume he was wearing an iron sword. Iron was a harder metal, stronger than brass. It also had a sharper edge, and was a lot more effective.

Rapha was probably one of the giants killed earlier in this chapter, and not being named. However, he could have died of natural causes, as other men died that way. He was only a man, (abnormal) subject to the same diseases and causes of death. One thing we know, he was not living. Since Goliath was the only remaining giant.

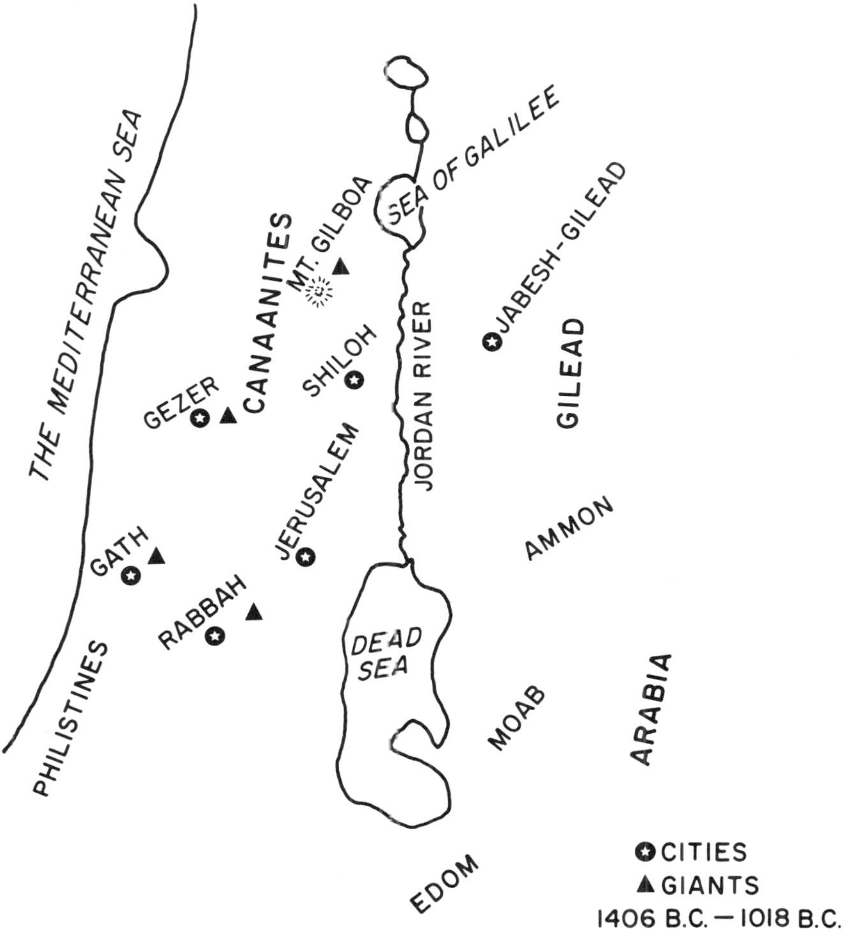
THE MEDITERRANEAN SEA
SEA OF GALILEE
JABESH-GILEAD
MT. GILBOA
CANAANITES
SHILOH
GEZER
JORDAN RIVER
GILEAD
JERUSALEM
AMMON
GATH
RABBAH
DEAD SEA
PHILISTINES
MOAB
ARABIA
EDOM
CITIES
GIANTS
1406 B.C. — 1018 B.C.

Map 7

CHAPTER NINE

Goliath

(1063 B.C.) Goliath is the most famous giant of all giants. We have taught about him in Sunday school classes from the cradle roll age to the senior adult classes, for generations. He is the great giant David slew with a small stone from his sling, when David was a very young person. From the story of his courage to face the enemy of God and his people, we build our courage to face our daily test. Some of our problems seem as large as a giant. Gath was the town where Goliath lived. It was a city in the land or country of Canaan. Goliath was not a Godly (good) man, but was a friend and companion of the Philistines. They were enemies of God's people, the Israelites. Goliath was the most famous giant of all. King Og was the second, most well-known. He had quite a reputation as the leader of the people in his kingdom.

Goliath was very large and powerful. He was six cubits and a span. A cubit was called twenty-one inches by some people of that age. Eighteen inches by other people. A span was from six to eight inches so he was either nine feet six inches tall, or eleven feet tall. He was a warrior of the Philistines. His breast plate weighed three hundred and fifty pounds. As large as he was, he still wore much protection from the spears and arrows of the smaller men who were his enemy. The Israelites ranged from five feet tall to five feet and five inches, some perhaps were eight or nine inches over five feet.

Goliath came from a scattered remnant of giants (people) taking refuge with the Philistines, after the dispersion by the Ammorites. They forced them out of their country.

If you have noticed, we go back in time from the end of the last chapter to pick up the story of David's younger life, before he was king, when he killed Goliath.

King Saul was in battle against the Philistines. The brothers of David were in the king's army. David was too young to go to war, he was a shepherd, caring for his father's sheep.

The Bible tells us in I Samuel 17:2: And Saul and the men of Israel were gathered together, and pitched by the Valley of Elah, and set in battle array aginst the Philistines Verse 3: And the Philistines stood on a mountain on the one side, and Israel stood on a mountain on the other side: and there was a valley between them. Verse 4: And there went out a champion out of the camp of the Philistines, named Goliath, of Gath, whose height was six cubits and a span. Verse 5: And He had on a helmet of brass upon his head, and he was armed with a coat of mail: and the weight of the coat was five thousand shekels of brass. Verse 6: And he had greaves of brass upon his legs, and a target of brass between his shoulders. Verse 7: And the staff of his spear was like a weaver's beam; and his spear's head weighed six hundred shekels of iron: and one bearing a shield went before him. Verse 8: And he stood and cried unto the armies of Israel, and said unto them, why are ye come out to set your battle in array? Am not I a Philistine, and ye servants of Saul? Choose you a man for you, and let him come down to me. Verse 9: If he be able to fight with me, and to kill me, then will we be your servants; but if I prevail against him, and kill him, then shall ye be our servants and serve us. Verse 10: And the Philistine said, I defy the armies of Israel this day: give me a man, that we may fight together. Verse 11: When Saul and all Israel heard those words of the Philistine, they were dismayed, and greatly afraid.

David's father Jesse had eight sons, three were in the army of Saul. These three were the oldest of the family. Their names were Eliah, Ahinadab, and Shammah. David was the youngest of the eight.

David was a shepherd for his father Jesse's sheep. This is why David is sometimes referred to as the shepherd king. He became king after Saul died. David lived at Bethlehem in (Judah) or Judeah.

The giant presented himself to Sauls army for forty days. Once each morning and once each evening.

Jesse became worried about his sons in the army. He called David to him, and told him to go see how they were. I Samuel 17:17: Jesse said unto David his son, take now for the brethren and Elah of this parched corn, and these ten loaves, and run to the camp to thy brethren. Verse 18: And carry these ten cheeses unto the captain of their thousand, and look how thy brethren fare, and take their pledge. Verse 19: Now Saul and they, and all the men of Israel, were in the Valley of Elah, fighting with the Philistines.

Jesse was of old age and unable to go see about the sons in the army. David could be spared from the chores by the other sons and servants in the household. I Samuel 17:20: David rose up early in the morning, and left the sheep with a keeper, and took and went, as Jesse had commanded him; and he came to the trench, as the host was going forth to the battle. Verse 22: And David left his carriage in the hand of the keeper of the carriage, and ran unto the army, and came and saluted his brethren. Verse 23: And as he talked with them, behold there came up the champion, the Philistine of Gath, Goliath by name, out of the armies of the Philistines, and spake according to the same words, and David heard them. Verse 24: And all the men of Israel, when they saw the man, fled from him and were sore afraid. Verse 26: And David spake to the man that stood by him, saying, what shall be done to the man that killeth this Philistine, and taketh away the reproach from Israel? For who is this uncircumcised Philistine, that he should defy the armies of the living God? Verse 28: And Eliah his eldest brother heard when he spake unto the men; and Eliah's anger was kindled against David, and he said, why camest thou down hither? And with whom hast thou left those few sheep in the wilderness? I know thy pride, and the naughtiness of thine heart; for thou art come down that thou mightest see the battle.

Verse 31: And when the words were heard which David spake, they rehearsed them before Saul, and he sent for him. Verse 32: And David said to Saul, let no man's heart fail because of him; thy servant will go and fight with this Philistine. Verse 33: And Saul said to David, thou are not able to go against this Philistine to fight with him, for thou art but a youth, and he a man of war from his youth. Verse 34: And David said unto Saul, thy servant kept his father's sheep, and there came a lion, and a bear and took a lamb out of the flock. Verse 35: And I went out after him, and smote him and delivered it out of his mouth, and when he arose against me, I caught him by his beard, and smote him and slew him. Verse 36: Thy servant slew both the lion and the bear; and this uncircumcised Philistine shall be as one of them, seeing he hath defiled the armies of the living God. Verse 37: David said moreover the Lord that delivered me out of the paw of the lion, and out of the paw of the bear, he will deliver me out of the hand of this Philistine. And Saul said unto David, go and the Lord be with thee.

Verse 40: And he (David) took his staff in his hand, and chose him five smooth stones out of the brook, and put them in a shepherd's bag which he had, even in a script, and his sling was in his hand, and he drew near to the Philistine. Verse 41: And the Philistine came on and drew near unto David; and the man that bear the shield went before him. Verse 42: And when the Philistine looked about, and saw David, he disdained him, for he was but a youth, and ruddy and of a fair countenance. Verse 43: And the Philistine said unto David, am I a dog, that thou comest to me with staves? And the Philistine cursed David by his Gods. Verse 44: And the Philistine said to David, come to me and I will give thy flesh unto the fowls of the air, and to the beast of the field. Verse 45: Then said David to the Philistine, thou comest to me with a sword, and with a spear, and with a shield, but I come to thee in the name of the Lord of Hosts, the God of the armies of Israel, whom thou defied. Verse 46: This day will the Lord deliver thee unto mine hand, and I will smite thee, and take thine head from thee, and I will give the carcases of the host of the Philistines this day unto the fowls of the air, and to the wild beast of the earth; that all may know that there is a God in Israel.

As mentioned earlier this is the early stage of iron coming into use, early stage of the iron age. As you read these verses describing the armor of Goliath, all the metal pieces of the armour was made of brass, except the spearhead, which was made of iron. Perhaps his sword was made of iron. Iron was much stronger and harder than brass, and kept a sharp edge longer. Goliath's gear and weapons were the latest known to warfare. He had the best of that age.

David used only the natural things God had created, smooth stones. Here we see a teenager, with a smooth face; he never had shaved. Ruddy (pink) of cheeks, defying the man who had defied David's God. With faith that his God would deliver him.

I Samuel 17:47: And all this assembly shall know that the Lord saveth not with swords and spear, for the battle is the Lord's, and he will deliver you unto your hands. Verse 48: And it came to pass, when the Philistine arose, and came and drew nigh to meet David, that David hasted, and ran toward the army to meet the Philistine. Verse 49: David put his hand in his bag, and took thence a stone, and slang it, and smote the Philistine in his forehead, and he fell upon his face to the earth. Verse 50: So David prevailed over the Philistine with a sling and with a stone, and smote the Philistine, and slew him, but there was no word in the hand of David. Verse 51: Therefore David ran, and stood upon the Philistine, and took his sword, and drew it out of the sheath thereof, and slew him, and cut off his head therewith. And when the Philistines saw their champion was dead, they fled. Verse 54: And David took the head of the Philistine, and brought it to Jerusalem, but he put the armor in his tent.

So we see the most famous, most colorful giant of all giants, was killed. David was royally rewarded for his brave deed. King Saul set him over the men of war. King Saul also gave his daughter Michal to be David's wife, thus he became son-in-law to the king. All the people in the kingdom loved David, because he had won the battle against their enemies. They now had peace.

King Saul became jealous of David, he turned against David and tried to kill David. David had to flee from the presence of the king. In 1062 B.C., David came to Nob to Ahimelech the priest. The priest asked David why he was alone. David told him, he was on a secret mission for the king. David was hungry, he asked the priest for some loaves of bread. The priest said there was no common bread around the place. It was forbidden for the holy bread of sacrifice to be eaten by anyone, but the priest. The priest said he had some hallowed bread there, that had been removed so fresh bread could be put in its place. Since David had not defiled himself with a woman for three days he was clean and holy. So the priest gave David hallowed bread, and he ate.

I Samuel 21:8: David said unto Ahimelech, and is there not here under thine hand spear or sword, for I have neither brought my sword or my weapons with me, because the King's business required haste. Verse 9: And the priest said, the sword of Goliath the Philistine, who thou slewest in the valley of Elah, behold it is here wrapped in a cloth behind the Ephod, if thou wilt take that, take it, for there is none other save that here. And David said there is none like that, give it me.

Again David was rewarded by receiving Goliath's sword. The sword was a reminder, God had given him victory over the giant, and now God would go with him in this new problem. God did give him strength, patience, and finally King Saul's kingdom.

Goliath's War Gear

Helmet of Brass	
Coat of Mail	312 lbs.
Breast Plate	350 lbs.
Back Target of Brass	
Greaves for Legs of Brass	
Spearhead of Iron	37 lbs.
Shield of Brass	
Sword of Iron	

Fig. 5 Goliath

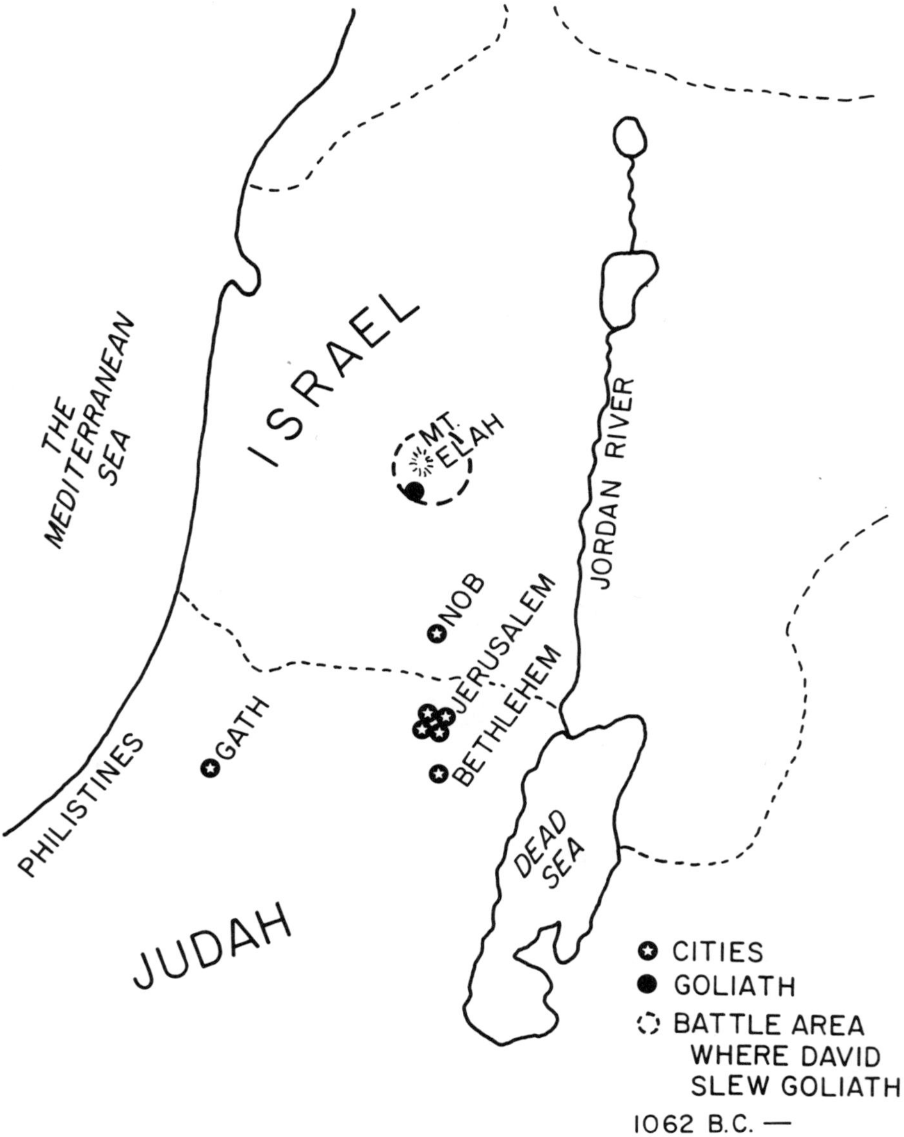
THE MEDITERRANEAN SEA
ISRAEL
MT. ELAH
JORDAN RIVER
NOB
JERUSALEM
BETHLEHEM
GATH
PHILISTINES
DEAD SEA
JUDAH
CITIES
GOLIATH
BATTLE AREA WHERE DAVID SLEW GOLIATH
1062 B.C. —

Map 8

CHAPTER TEN

Ezra's Instruction to Benjamin

Because Benjamin and his offspring had sinned against God, and had taken wives from the ungodly, forbidden races of people around him, God sent a message to his tribe through Ezra the prophet.

This last race of giants was sent as a curse against the Benjaminites. God said men were evil continually before him. The land had become so polluted by sin, few Godly men survived.

God cleansed the land through David and his armies, that his people the Israelites might live a holy life in the new land of promise. Moses, Joshua, and Caleb had led the Israelites from Goshen in Egypt to the place God gave them.

By 1018 B.C., God had removed all the giants from the land. This curse had been removed from God's children, never to come upon them again.

Still the people did not worship God in love, with honor, as God desired, neither did they keep the commandments of the law. In 586 B.C., God allowed their temple to be destroyed, and the mass of the people were taken to Babylon as captives, and slaves by King Nebuchadnezzar. God still had to punish them for their sins.

In 536 B.C. King Cyrus allowed the Jews to return to Jerusalem from Babylon, to rebuild their city. God had allowed the people to be in bondage that they might repent, call upon him and return to worship him, with heartfelt love and their sacrifices.

God had always used a prophet to help the people unite with him. Ezra was the prophet for that time in history. Ezra told the people to repent of their sins, and God would give them the message of his will for them.

When the people cried in thir bondage, God heard their cries. They longed for their homeland, their city and their temple. God worked upon the heart of the king, to allow them to return and rebuild their city. Ezra also was allowed to lead the people as they returned.

(536 B.C.) In this year they did return, to start the work of rebuilding. They were in Jerusalem three days and made a grat sacrifice to God. At this time God showed Ezra the priest how sinful the people still were.

Ezra 9:1: Now when these things were done, the princes came to me, saying, the people of Israel, and the priest and the Levites, have not separated themselves from the people of the lands, doing according to their abominations, even of the Canaanites, the Hittites, the Perizzites, the Jehusites, the Ammonites, the Moabites, the Egyptians and the Amorites. Verse 2: For they have taken their daughters for themselves, and for their sons; so the holy seed have mingled themselves with the people of the lands: yea, the hand of the prince and the rulers hath been chief in this transpass. Verse 3: And when I heard this thing, I rent my garment and mantle and plucked the hair of my head and of my beard, and sat down astonished. Verse 4: Then were assembled unto me every one that trembled at the words of the God of Israel, because of the transgression of those that had been carried away; and I sat astonished until the evening sacrifice. Verse 5: And at the evening sacrifice I arose up from my heaviness, and having rent my garment and my mantle, I fell upon my knees, and spread out my hands unto the Lord my God. Verse 6: And said, "My God, I am ashamed to blush to lift up my face to thee, My God, for our iniquities are increased over our head, and our trespass is grown up unto the heavens."

Ezra 10:1: Now when Ezra had prayed, and when he had confessed, weeping and casting himself down before the house of God there assembled unto him out of Israel a very great congregation of men and women and children, for the people wept very sore. Verse 2: And Shechaniah the son of Jehiel, one of the sons of Elam, answered and said unto Ezra we have trespassed against our God, and have taken strange wives of the people of the land, yet now there is hope in Israel concerning this thing. Verse 3: Now, therefore, let us make a covenant with our God, to put away all the wives, and such as are born of them, according to the counsel of my Lord, and of those that tremble at the commandment of our God, and let it be done according to the law.

Ezra told the people to be of good courage, and swear to do the commandments of the Lord. Then Ezra went before the house of God, and ate no food or drink water. For he mourned for the transgression of them that had been carried away.

Verse 7: And they made proclamation throughout Judah and Jerusalem unto all the children of captivity, that they should gather themselves together at Jerusalem. Verse 8: And that whosoever would not come within three days, according to the counsel of the princes and the elders, all his substance should be forfeited, and himself separated from the congregation of those that had been carried away.

Verse 9: Then all the men of Judah and Benjamin gathered themselves together unto Jerusalem within three days. Verse 10: And Ezra the priest stood up and said unto them, ye have transgressed, and have taken strange wives, to increase the trespass of Israel. Verse 11: And, therefore, make confession unto the Lord God of your fathers, and do his pleasure, and separate yourselves from the people of the land, and from the strange wives. Verse 12: Then all the congregation answered and said with a loud voice, as thou hast said, so must we do.

The men of Benjamin had repented and obeyed God's command, and we see an end come to the transgression. This transgression was why God had caused the giants to be born, as a curse in earlier times, to this tribe of Benjamin.

The giants of this book began in 4004 B.C. and ended in 1018 B.C. The cause of giants had not ended the sins that their fathers had committed. God ended the curse, and dealt with men in some other manner, in later time.

Thanks be to our God that has preserved his living and inspiring word (the Bible), from which we have taken these very interesting facts about the giants of the Bible. It has been very thrilling to follow these giant people from their origin to their end.

CHAPTER ELEVEN

Giants of Our Day

Although we do not have giant men to contend with today, we do have some moral, mental, and spiritual giants to overcome in our everyday lives. Let us look at some of them.

GIANT NUMBER ONE

In our society we expect and are expected to live like kings and queens. We strive to live in large houses, attractive and well decorated. We want the best furniture of the period we choose to enjoy. Not to mention the landscape yards and the push button electrical conveniences. Sheets ever so soft with color-coordinating towels, blankets and rugs, etc.

Jewelry of the best quality, gold, silver, diamonds and precious gems. There is no end to the array. Time pieces you never have to wind or set. Everything precision to perfection.

There is also the realm of automobiles. A large percentage of families in the world own and operate from one to six vehicles, for family use, work or pleasure. To apply our most concentrated efforts to achieve all of these things and more. They must be equal or better than our neighbor's possessions.

We desire animals of high pedigree, telling the value of our dog, cat, or horse, etc., before we tell his name and breed.

Then how about our dress. The best quality and fashion we can afford. Many, many hundreds of dollars spent each year on grooming of the hair and toiletries. We look and smell like kings and queens.

The wives are expected to look like a beauty pageant queen. And to act like royalty,—gracious at all times. She must be a thrilling romantic partner to her husband, a good cook and devoted mother to their children. The house always neat and inviting.

While, on the side, she holds down a regular eight hour job, to supply her part of the payment for all these things she and her husband desire. But. . .there is always that striving to please her husband to keep him from turning to a more attractive female, of which there always seem to be a great number available.

Then there is the husband, who is expected to be capable of acquiring a high position and bring home a vast wage. He must be well educated and well groomed to do so. Always the competition to fulfill these areas of his life, by maintaining a self reliable status. There is that nagging in his mind; he must excel. He is to be a real champ in the golf or tennis game with friends and fellow workers. Also his duties to his wife's needs, love, admiration, and male fulfillment. He must never, never be too tired!

There always seems to be something extra to strive for, higher wages, shorter working hours and more time demanded for fellowship with his amily; he must stay healthy, eager and congenial. Do not let down! But most of all, there is the fear his beautiful wife will lose interest in him and start looking for someone more exciting. Fear the children might go astray, becoming involved in great problems.

Both husband and wife are taxed, strained and pressured to the very breaking point. "This giant is expecting too much." Not allowing relaxation that one might live a normal life, as God planned for man. Stop! Think! Slow down! It's a mortal battle for humans to whip this giant. (Covetousness.)

GIANT NUMBER TWO

It seems there is no honesty left in the world. We have learned to keep a protective wall up and be very suspicious in business deals, deals with friends or even family matters.

People take advantage of everything, for power, fame, money or gain of any kind. Old people are taken advantage of because they cannot perceive the crooks who will cheat them. Children are cheated also. It has come to an age when parents lie to children; lots of promises but never the time to fulfill them. Parents do not take time to love their children, care for them and teach them the true values of life. Aged parents are lied to by some adult children. Often no honor or respect is shown them. Parents cannot trust their children dealing in serious matters. Many are left on the street (sidewalk), so to speak, for some charity to care for.

How about partners in business? They cannot be trusted to keep their agreements. The sly, crafty one will cheat the naive.

Neighbors are at each other's throats over misunderstandings, property, pets, wives, (husbands), and children problems. Borrowing and lending become battlegrounds also.

There are the business contracts, with such small print one cannot read it. The small print is longer and harder to undestand each year.

If you are taken to court, you cannot depend on friends to back you up in the truth. There seems to be a price for their testimony, from your enemy. Today a man's word seems to be of no value, without proof. In earlier days deals were made by a handshake. No signed contracts.

What is this second giant we have to deal with today? "It is a false witness or lying."

GIANT NUMBER THREE

You cannot leave your house unlocked, or thieves will enter and remove all your furniture and valuable items, TVs, radios, guns, jewelry, clothing, money, etc. Your garage must also be locked, or the auto, bicycles, tools, and other valuables will be removed and hauled away.

Fences to keep your children and pets enlcosed. Not that they might get out, but to keep the enemy out. They will be spirited away, for ransom, sensual molesting, or murder.

On guard! On guard! At all times. It is not enough people have to work, to purchase the necessittes of life, they have to keep a constant vigil, to keep it. What is this third giant we strive with? "Dishonesty and stealing."

GIANT NUMBER FOUR

Even in the highest regarded families it seems scandals are exposed. The husband is having an affair with a woman, other than his legal wife. The grass is always greener on the other side of the fence. More fun, new experiences and more fulfillment. It seems he has such a drive for new pleasures nothing can restrain him. If others in his family cannot or will not tolerate his waywardness, he will just walk out; leaving all former status.

On the other hand many wives are tired of the same old game and are eager to pursue a new love affair, outside their legal boundary. The new man of interest is so flattering; after all he does appreciate her beauty and talents. He does not take her for granted! He has told her, how much pleasure she gives him. That she is too beautiful and youthful to be tied down at home, with a demanding husband and selfish children.

The two of them just need to hide away more often. If the family will not tolerate her waywardness she simply walks out, deserting the whole family, even the children who love and depend upon her. What is this fourth giant of today? Could it be "adultery?"

GIANT NUMBER FIVE

This giant has grown to be a very large thing to overcome: degeneration. Life seems of no value. Little children and old people are abandoned, left with no protection. Whereupon this evil, bloodthirsty giant attacks and takes their lives. Other persons, teen-agers and adults of all ages are also deprived of their lives. Many deaths are gruesome, cruel situations. Many are strangers to the murders which are without reason or purpose.

Countries kill many in wasteful, ruthless wars. It seems to be an age when the value of human life has been lost. No respect for anyone; many times there is no feeling of guilt, when one person kills another.

God has given each individual one life. If it is taken from them, it can never be reclaimed in the natural life. Then who is this fifth giant of a beast? "It's a robber of life, a killer."

GIANT NUMBER SIX

Respect or disrespect, this is the question. For whom? For parents!

In olden times when children were growing up, from childhood to adulthood, they were taught to honor their parents, and expected to do so. Therefore the children never refused to accept the decisions parents made for the family welfare. To be part of that family was an honor. To have the family name was respected. When the parents became too aged to maintain the family welfare, the oldest son would take charge of the management of the family as a whole. Loving and cherishing the aged, helpless parents until their death.

Today is a rebellious age, even small children refuse to be told what is best for them. In many families this type of child is allowed to run and roam around the neighborhood and city. When they are older they roam over the country, making their own decisions to live by. That is why a lot of problems occur causing the ever growing generation gap.

Much suffering comes to the parents and other family members, as well as to the rebellious youth themselves. Satan takes advantage of their being outside the family protection. He deals very harshly with them, often taking the life of the very young.

Who is this sixth terrible giant? "It's dishonor to parents."

GIANT NUMBER SEVEN

This giant robs us of as much or more than any of the other giants, whom we must fight and overcome. In our working patterns and laws of our land, each laborer is given one day each week off from his duties, to rest and refresh himself. That he may be able physically and mentally (as well as spiritually) to do a good job when he returns to his job agreement. But how many people rest on their rest day? Most people use the rest day to go to some pleasure spot, to push themselves until a very few hours before returning to their duties, usually exhausted and dull, making more errors than they like to admit. Without rest one becomes vrery nervous. After a long time of no rest one become mentally and physically ill.

Other problems such as frustration, heart attacks, nervous breakdown, stomach ulcers, high blood pressure, bad teeth and weak eyesight appear.

The human body needs rest and sleep, just as much as water, food and protection from the elements.

Man has taken his own life into his own hands, by making his own laws for his delicate body, refusing God's laws. What is this seventh giant we battle with each week? "No rest on the Sabbath Day."

GIANT NUMBER EIGHT

Sometimes this giant starts to grow in our speech habits from a very young age. Even small children use language learned from parents that is unacceptable to God and our own society. The children many times do not even know the meanings of the words they use.

These bywords and curse words are derived from a few root words of an insult to, and cursing the nane of God. This giant of bad language is degrading to the speaker and to the hearer

Cursing has caused a low profile in moral and spiritual areas of our life. Business is damaged. The home life is undermined, and friends begin to shun the curser. Many times friendships are lost.

Where do these persons end up? Usually with other base-thinking and speaking people of very low degeree. Far! Far! from God. God will not fellowship or bless anyone who uses his name in vain. "This giant number eight is irreverent cursing."

GIANT NUMBER NINE

What are the people of the world worshipping as their God today? Is our worship given to a deserving God? Think about it!

Sometimes idols of human beings receive worship. Sometimes it may be an idol or figure of an animal. Then there are the sun, moon, and stars. Some give their love and endeavors to these. How about Satan? For centuries images of Satan, monkeys, snakes, lions, crocodiles, and various things have been worshipped as Gods. It tells us in the Bible people worshipped "Nehusthan," the brazen serpent Moses lifted upon a pole. Hundreds of years later God had it destroyed, because his people were worshipping the idol of "Nehusthan" instead of his creator God. You can read about this in 2 Kings 18:14.

This ninth giant of replacing true worship of God to images is a distrous thing. "It is called graven idol worship."

GIANT NUMBER TEN

Now we have the greatest giant of our day to cope with. Where do we direct our lives and adoration of worship? Are we fooling ourselves in giving our time, strength and devotion false values.?

Satan will make the copy of the real thing so much like it, sometimes it takes very close attention to detect the counterfeit.

Where is our time involved? Making a success in our own abilities? Going to the limit of our own strength? Investing our time and talents into something we make a God to ourselves? Forgetting God in Heaven is due our first (best) love and devotion. He should be our guide, our master and our father.

When we have exhausted our own abilities we realize we have been pampering, feeding, and defending the counterfeit and have lost the real thing.

Oh! How much our lives have been wasted. Can we make a new commitment to God, with a new vision of Him? He loves his children, and cares for them with tender care. Will we completely put him first in all our ways, that he might be pleased? So what is this last and tenth modern giant of our day? "It is a substitute for God."

I'm sure by now you have realized what these ten giants are; they are what God knew would become giant problems to us, his people of all ages. They are the ten commandments turned upside down or reversed from last to first. That the most important one would be the last and strongest of all. If we will live by them as God intended, we have whipped the giants of today, by keeping the first commandment; all the others are included.

The Ten Commandments listed in next chapter.

CHAPTER TWELVE

God's Law Erases Our Giants of Today

Exodus 20:1-7 verse 1: "And God spake all these words, saying. Verse 2: I am the Lord thy God, which have brought thee out of the land of Egypt, out of the house of bondage."

I

Verse 3: Thou shalt have no other Gods before me.

II

Verse 4: Thou shalt not make unto thee any graven image, or any likeness of anything that is in Heaven above, or that is in the earth beneath, or that is in the water under the earth.
Verse 5: Thou shalt not bow down thyself to them, nor serve them, for I the Lord God am a jealous God, visiting the iniquity of the fathers upon the children unto the third and fourth generations of them that hate me.
Verse 6: Showing mercy unto thousands of them that love me, and keep my commandments.

III

Verse 7: Thou shalt not take the name of the Lord thy God in vain, for the Lord will not hold him guiltless that taketh his name in vain.

IV

Verse 8: Remember the Sabbath Day to keep it holy.
Verse 9: Six days shalt thou labor, and do all thy work.
Verse 10: But the seventh day is the Sabbath of the Lord thy God, in it thou shalt not do any work, thou nor thy son, nor thy daughter, thy man-servant, nor thy maid-servant, nor thy cattle, nor thy stranger that is within thy gates.
Verse 11: For in six days the Lord made Heaven and earth, the sea and all that in them is, and rested the seventh day, wherefore the lord blessed the Sabbath Day and hallowed it.

V

Verse 12: Honor thy father and thy mother, that thy days may be long upon the land which the lord thy God giveth thee.

VI

Verse 13: Thou shalt not kill.

VII

Verse 14: Thou shalt not commit adultery.

VIII

Verse 15: Thou shalt not steal.

IX

> Verse 16: Thou shalt not bear false witness against thy neighbor.

X

> Verse 17: Thou shalt not covet thy neighbor's house, thou shalt not covet thy neighbor's wife, nor his man-servant, nor his maid-servant, nor his ox, nor his ass, nor anything that is thy neighbor's.

What is our victory and peace in this life? It is love. The Bible tells us "God is love." John 3:16: For God so loved the world he gave his only begotten son, that whosoever believeth in him should not perish, but have everlasting life.

You see if we love God, we will love his son. If we love his son we will love our fellow men. On love hinges peace for us in the U.S.A. and all other nations of the world.

The Bible tells us in II Chronicles 7:14: "If my people which are called by my name, shall humble themselves, and pray, and seek my face, and turn from their wicked ways; then will I hear from Heaven, and will forgive their sins, and will heal their land."

Also in the New Testament in John 13:3–4: "A new commandment I give unto you, that ye love one another, as I have loved you, that ye also love one another."

Until we can love one another, without criticism in our dealings, God cannot accept our love to him. Only through his help can we have this perfect love for others.

If we have problems, large or small, we will find help and an answer to deal with them effectively in the inspired word of God. "The Bible." A declaration of love.